KAREN BROWN'S

Italian

Country Bed & Breakfasts

To Carole & Susan,

My favorite Italian travel book for my favorite travel companions!

Patricia 4/94

ITALIAN FARMER'S POEM

Our memories are crouched
in silence within the belly of the earth.
Yet it takes only a day of sunshine,
an impromptu storm in the sky,
the perfume of freshly cut hay,
and immense fields dotted with golden haystacks,
to ignite in us the memories
of certain evenings spent full of gaiety.

It was at sunset when we used to join together
in the barn filled with grain
to celebrate the end of the harvest.
The "gioanassa" musician friend,
pressing the keys of his worn-out accordion,
succeeding in emitting the notes
to a waltz or mazurka, leaving us
drunk with happiness.

One more glass of wine before the night
fades into day.
One more toast to bid farewell
to another summer
that crossed the path of our youth.

Anonymous

KAREN BROWN'S

Italian Country Bed & Breakfasts

Written by

NICOLE FRANCHINI

Illustrations by Elisabetta Franchini

Cover Painting by Jann Pollard

Travel Press
Karen Brown's Country Inn Series

KAREN BROWN TITLES

California Country Inns & Itineraries

English Country Bed & Breakfasts

English, Welsh & Scottish Country Hotels & Itineraries

French Country Bed & Breakfasts

French Country Inns & Itineraries

German Country Inns & Itineraries

Irish Country Inns & Itineraries

Italian Country Bed & Breakfasts

Italian Country Inns & Itineraries

Spanish Country Inns & Itineraries

Swiss Country Inns & Itineraries

To
Carlo and Livia,
With all my Love

Editors: Nicole Franchini, Susanne Lau Alloway, Karen Brown, June Brown, Clare Brown
Illustrations: Elisabetta Franchini, Cover painting: Jann Pollard
Maps: Susanne Lau Alloway—Greenleaf Design & Graphics

Written in cooperation with Town & Country-Hillsdale Travel, San Mateo, CA 94401

Distributed USA & Canada: The Globe Pequot Press; tel: (203) 395-0440, fax: (203) 395-0312
Box 833, Old Saybrook, CT 06475-0833, U.S.A.

Distributed Europe: Springfield Books Ltd.; tel: (0484) 864 955, fax: (0484) 865 443
Norman Road., Denby Dale, Huddersfield HD8 8TH, W. Yorkshire, England
A catalog record for this book is available from the British Library

Distributed Australia: Little Hills Press Pty. Ltd.; tel: (02) 437-6995, fax: (02) 438-5762
1st Floor, Regent House, 37-43 Alexander St, Crows Nest NSW 2065, Australia

Distributed New Zealand: Tandem Press Ltd.; tel: (0064) 9 480-1452, fax: (0064) 9 480 1455
P.O. Box 34-272, Birkenhead, Auckland 10, New Zealand

Library of Congress Cataloging-in-Publication Data

Franchini, Nicole, 1959-
    Italian country bed & breakfasts / written by Nicole Franchini;
sketches by Elisabetta Franchini, cover painting by Jann Pollard
        p. cm. -- (Karen Brown's country inn series)
    Rev. 2nd ed. of: Karen Brown's Italian country bed & breakfasts.
    Includes index.
    ISBN 0-930328-24-8 ; $14.95
-Guidesbooks. I. Franchini, Nicole, 1959- Karen Brown's Italian
country bed & breakfasts. II. Title. III. Title: Italian country
bed and breakfasts. IV. Series.
TX 907.5.I8F73   1994   93-30061
647.944503--dc20   CIP

Contents

Introduction

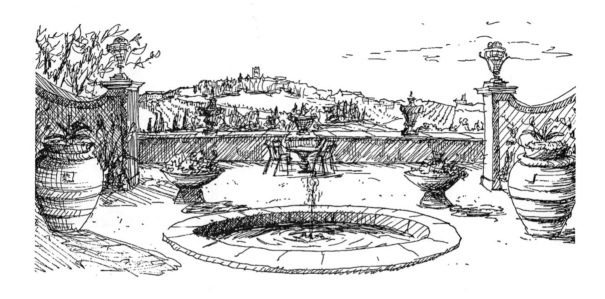

BED AND BREAKFAST ITALIAN-STYLE—*agriturismo*, as the bed and breakfast activity is called in Italy, has made great strides over the past decade. The B&B concept is relatively new to Italy, which followed suit after France and England originated the Bed & Breakfast trend. Accommodations vary from simple farmhouses to noble country villas, all promising unique and memorable stays.

Agritourism travel offers visitors to Italy the unique opportunity to observe daily life "up close" as a guest in someone's home. It is a superb way to interact directly with Italians, experiencing their way of life as a participant rather than just an observer. It offers a more intimate contact with the country's traditional ways of life than can ever be experienced during hotel stays. It is the alternative vacation for curious visitors who wish to explore the back roads of this fascinating country and depart with a more in-depth understanding of Italians and their lifestyles than they could possibly get from city stays and sightseeing alone. The individual who will benefit most from agritourism will have an open, inquiring mind and a certain amount of flexibility. In return, agritourism rewards the traveler with a feeling of being "at home" while abroad. The warm welcome and the value you'll receive may bring you back to the agritourism track year after year.

Called *agriturismo* in Italian, this term is defined as agricultural tourism, and was founded in 1965 as part of the Italian government's national agricultural department. Its objective was to make it possible for farmers to supplement their declining income in two ways: through offering accommodation to tourists and through direct sales of their produce.

After World War II, during reconstruction and the subsequent industrial boom, Italians abandoned the countryside in droves in search of employment in urban centers, reducing the rural population from eight to three-million people. Consequently, farmhouses, villas and castles all across the country were neglected and went to ruin. This phenomenon also disrupted the centuries-old tradition of passing customs and property from one generation to the next.

The agritourism concept, with its government funding and proclaimed tax breaks, has lured proprietors back to their land and ancestral homes, providing them with the incentive to restore and preserve these historical buildings (with many treasures among them), without spoiling the natural landscape. An additional consequence is an improved distribution of tourism between Italy's overcrowded cities and the countryside that serves to raise awareness of the many marvelous attractions, from art and architecture to scenery and cuisine, that await tourists off the beaten track.

Each of Italy's twenty regions participates in agritourism, with a full 60% of participants concentrated in Tuscany and Trentino Alto Adige. This second edition of *Italian Country Bed & Breakfasts* includes selections from twelve of Italy's regions. Unfortunately, this type of accommodation is still very scarce in Italy's southern-most regions such as Sicily, Calabria, Basilicata, and Campania.

In practical terms, agritourism was developed to stimulate the local economy in rural areas, by encouraging the creation of accommodation (rooms, apartments and campgrounds) in places where they had never before been available. In a more long-term and idealistic sense, it was hoped that the promotion and development of tourism in rural Italy would also bring about greater environmental awareness and rescue traditional folklore and customs, as regional cuisine and handicrafts from oblivion, and for posterity.

For Italians, agritourism facilitates an exchange of views between farmers and urbanites who come in search of a peaceful vacation surrounded by natural beauty. In fact, agritourism and the rich culture of the farmer represent for many an affirmation and validation of their heritage. Lamentably, some Italians have a misconception of agritourism because it was originally organized as an exchange of very basic room and board for work in the fields. So there remains today an unfortunate lack of awareness of the variety of accommodation (from simple farmhouse to elaborate castle) available through the associations, and agritourism has not flourished to its potential.

Controversy also surrounds the fact that there are few established regulations governing this type of activity, and they differ greatly from one region to another. Consequently, no clearly defined quality standards exist and those participants with limited economic resources resent wealthier proprietors, whom they accuse of running accommodations resembling hotels more than farm stays.

Moreover, it doesn't simplify matters that agritourism is organized in typical Italian fashion, with responsibility divided among three associations, each with its own regulations, politics and guidelines. Each association produces a directory (in Italian), and may be contacted by writing to:

AGRITURIST, Corso Vittorio Emanuele 101, Rome 00168, Italy

TERRANOSTRA, Via 14 Maggio 43, Rome 00187, Italy

TURISMO VERDE, Via M. Fortuny 20, Rome 00196, Italy

ACCOMMODATION

Descriptions: Agritourism accommodation should not be thought of strictly in terms of the British definition of bed and breakfasts, as in Italy they vary greatly according to each proprietor's interpretation of the concept. The B&Bs in this guide have been described in terms of the criteria used in their selection—warmth of hospitality, historic character, charm of the home, scenery, proximity to sites of touristic interest, and quality of cuisine. Obviously, all of these attributes are not always found in each B&B. Most B&B's have an average of six rooms that are situated either within the family's home or in a separate guest house. We have tried to include only those with ensuite bathrooms, as per our reader's request (although for the budget traveler this may not be a priority). Since more and more travelers are learning that it is much more advantageous to stay for longer periods in one place (distances are so short between towns within a specific region), apartment-type accommodations with fully-equipped kitchenettes are flourishing. And in fact, jumping around from one place to another for one or two nights defeats the purpose of a more intimate contact with host families.

APARTMENTS: Apartment accommodation is offered either within the farmhouse along with other units for 2-4 persons, or as a full house rental for 4-8 persons. They are rented by the week from Saturday to Saturday throughout the country. No meals are included unless the B&B also has a restaurant. Rates include use of all facilities, unless otherwise indicated, linens and cleaning once a week. There is usually an extra charge for heating.

FOOD: A highlight of the agritourism experience is without a doubt the food. Most travelers would agree that a bad meal is hard to find in Italy, a country world-famous for its culinary skills. In the countryside you'll be sampling the traditional recipes from which Italian cuisine originates. Seeing that whenever possible all of the ingredients come directly from the farms where you'll be staying, you'll discover the flavorful difference freshness can make. A peek into the farm kitchen is likely to reveal pasta being rolled and cut the old-fashioned way—by hand. Many country cooks prefer to prepare food using traditional methods, and not rely on machines to speed up the process. Guests are usually welcomed into the kitchen for a peek and actual cooking lessons are becoming very popular.

LANGUAGE: English spoken at each B&B has been indicated as follows: fluent, very well, well, some, little or none. We would like to note, however, that this is just an indication, as the person who speaks English may or may not be there during your stay. In any case, it is helpful (not to mention rewarding) to have a few basic Italian phrases on hand. A phrase book or dictionary is indispensable. And when all else fails, the art of communicating with gestures is still very much alive in Italy!

LENGTH OF STAY: Agriturismo is most advantageous for those who have more than the standard one week to travel. Bed and breakfast accommodations take longer to reach, for one thing, plus OFTEN THEY ARE NEITHER SET UP NOR STAFFED FOR ONE-NIGHT STAYS, which increase costs and defeat the purpose. There are numerous exceptions, however, especially in B&Bs near cities, where overnight guests are accepted. It is noted in the description where a minimum stay is required.

MEALS OFFERED: B&Bs sometime serve breakfast only, most often coffee, tea, fresh breads and jams. However, many prepare other meals, as well, and offer (sometimes require) half or full-board plans. Half board means that breakfast and dinner are both included in the daily per-person room rate. Full board rate includes the room and all three meals and is less common, since most guests are out and about during the day, or prefer one lighter meal. Dinner is a hearty three-course meal, often shared at a common table with the host family, and usually includes wine. Menus might be set daily, according to the availability of fresh produce, or a limited choice may be given. Other times a farm will have a full-fledged restaurant serving non-guests as well. So that travelers who are not necessarily guests at a particular B&B may take advantage of the opportunity to sample other fare, B&Bs with restaurants are distinguished by the term "All meals served." It is advisable to reserve in advance. "Trattoria on premises" indicates a restaurant that exists as a separate function to the B&B.

RATES: Room rates vary according to size, season and level of service and luxury. Rates range from $50 to $200 for a double room with breakfast (indicated as B&B in the following descriptions) and from $35 to $100 per person for room with half board. The majority of the B&Bs selected for this guide have private bathrooms. APPROXIMATE PRICES FOR 1994 ARE INDICATED IN LIRE AND ARE BY NO MEANS FIXED.

Rates include tax and breakfast unless otherwise indicated, and are CONFIRMED AT TIME OF RESERVATION. Credit cards are rarely accepted, cash being the preferred method of payment. When "plastic payment" is taken, the type of card accepted will be indicated as follows: AX: American Express; DC: Diner's Club, MC: Master Card; VS: Visa; or all major. Because of its cost advantages, agritourism is an ideal choice for a family vacation. Children under eight are offered a discount and hosts will almost always add an extra bed for a small charge.

RESERVATIONS: Whether you plan to stay in several B&Bs or decide to remain for an extended period in just one, ADVANCE RESERVATIONS ARE PREFERRED. Not only do many of the B&Bs have only a few bedrooms available, but also they are usually in private homes that are not prepared to take walk-in traffic. There are several ways to make a reservation:

Fax: A few places to stay (especially in or near cities) have fax numbers. Faxing is a quick way to make a reservation (remember to include your fax number for their response). A reservation request letter in Italian with an English translation is on page 185.

Letter: You can write to the B&B (allow up to six weeks for an answer because mail to Italy is very slow). If you have plenty of time and decide to write, make photocopies of the sample reservation-request letter (on page 185) written in Italian with an English translation. (Note: In correspondence, be sure to spell out the month.) Frequently a deposit is requested in order to confirm the reservation.

Reservation Service: If you want to pay for the convenience of having the reservations made for you, pre-payments made, vouchers issued and cars rented, any of the B&Bs in this guide can be booked through HIDDEN TREASURES OF ITALY, a booking service run by the author of this guide, Nicole Franchini. Further information as to the charges and the request form are found at the back of this book.

Telephone: You can call the B&B directly. This is very efficient since you will get an immediate response. (The level of English spoken is given in each B&B description.) To telephone Italy from the United States, dial 011 (the international code), then 39 (Italy's code), then the city code (dropping the 0), and the telephone number. Allow for the time difference in Italy which is six hours ahead of New York.

Travel agent: You can ask your travel agent to assist you with your reservations. Be aware that most travel agents will charge for their services since it is time consuming to make reservations and most places to stay in this guide are too small to pay any commission to compensate for the costs involved.

TYPE OF SERVICE: The most important thing to remember as you consider an agritourism vacation is that you will be staying in the private homes of families that are obligated to run their B&Bs without hiring additional personnel aside from family and farmhands. Do not forget that, in most cases, the primary responsibility of your hosts is the running of their farm. So, with a few exceptions, do not expect the service of a hotel. Nevertheless, do anticipate a comfortable and enjoyable stay, because the proprietors will do everything possible to assure it. Cost will vary according to the level of service offered. (For the traveler's convenience, some city hotels have been included that are similar to a B&B in style, but go by the name *Albergo*, *Pensione* or Hotel.)

WHAT TO SEE AND DO: B&B proprietors take pride in their farms and great pleasure in answering questions about their agricultural activity. They will often take time to explain and demonstrate procedures such as wine making, olive pressing or cheese production. They are the best source for, and are happy to suggest restaurants, local itineraries, including historic sites, picturesque villages and cultural activities. Your B&B hosts feel responsible for entertaining their guests and many have added swimming pools or tennis courts if they are not already available in the vicinity. Other activities such as archery, fishing, hiking and biking are sometimes offered. Horseback riding has made an enormous comeback and farms frequently have their own stables and organize lessons and/or excursions into the countryside.

BANKS

Banking hours are Monday through Friday from 8:30 am to 1:30 pm and 3:00 pm to 4:00 pm. *Cambio* signs outside and inside a bank indicate that it will exchange traveler's checks or give you cash from certain credit cards. Also privately-run exchange offices are available in cities with more convenient hours and comparable rates.

DRIVING IN ITALY

DRIVER'S LICENSE: The International Driver's Permit is not necessary for stays less than six months, and when renting a car. An oversea's driver's license is valid for driving throughout Italy, which is not quite the "vehicular-free-for-all" you may've heard about, at least not outside big cities (particularly Rome, Florence and Milan). When visiting Rome, it's advisable to do so at the beginning or end of your trip, before you pick up or after you drop off your car, and by all means, avoid driving within the city. Italians have a different relationship with the basic rules of the road. Common maneuvers include running stop lights and stop signs, triple parking, driving 100 mph on the highways, passing on the right, and backing up at missed highway exits. But once out of the city, you will find it relatively easy to reach your destination. Road directions are quite good in Italy and people are very willing to help.

DISTANCES: Distances are indicated in kilometers (one km equals 0.621 miles), calculated roughly into miles by cutting the kilometer distance in half. Distances between towns are also indicated in orange alongside the roads on the Touring Club Italiano maps. Italy is a compact country and distances are relatively short, yet you will be amazed at how dramatically the scenery can change in an hour's drive.

GAS COUPONS: Foreigners often are confused about gas coupons (maybe because the rules change every six months or so). Available only to tourists, these coupons can be purchased at national borders and from the automobile club of Italy (ACI) upon arrival at either the Milan or Rome airport. The savings are up to 20% and include tollway vouchers and free breakdown service. Coupons can be refunded at the place of purchase. Packets are sold according to your area of destination: northern, central or southern Italy.

GASOLINE–PRICES: Gas prices in Italy are the highest in Europe, and Americans often suspect a mistake when their first fill up comes to $45 to $80 (most of it in taxes). Some stations now accept *Visa* credit cards, and the ERG stations accept American Express. Besides the AGIP stations on the autostrade, which are almost always open, gas stations observe the same hours as merchants, closing in the afternoon from 12:30 to 4:00 pm and in the evening at 7:30. Be careful not to get caught running on empty in the afternoon! Many stations have a self-service pump that operates on off-hours, and accepts only 10,000 lire bills. WARNING: At tollway gas stations and snack bars, always lock your car and beware of gypsies and vendors who try to sell you stolen merchandise. This practice is most prevalent south of Rome. In general, NEVER leave valuables or even luggage in the car. Also, NEVER set down luggage even for a minute in train stations.

MAPS: An above-average map of Italy is absolutely essential for this type of travel. The Touring Club Italiano maps, in an easy-to-read three-volume format divided into North,

Central and South, is a superior selection. Even the smallest town or better, *localita* is indicated in the extensive index. In addition, places of particular interest are underlined or boxed in green, as are exceptionally scenic roads. Another fine choice are the Rand McNally *Hallwag* maps. Depending upon your itinerary, you need either their map of "Northern Italy" or "Southern Italy," or both (the whole-country map isn't specific enough). Each comes with a small index booklet to help you locate the towns.

ROADS: Names of roads in Italy are as follows:

Autostrada: a large, fast (and most direct) two or three-lane tollway, marked by green signs bearing an "A" followed by the autostrada number. A ticket is issued by an automatic machine upon entrance. Speed limit: 130 kph.

Superstrada: a one or two-lane freeway between secondary cities marked by blue signs and given a number. Speed limit: 110 kph.

Strada statale: a small one-lane road marked with S.S. followed by the road number. Speed limit: 90 kph.

Raccordo or *Tangenziale*: a ring road around main cities, connecting to autostrada and city centers.

ROAD SIGNS: Yellow signs are for tourists and indicate a site of historical or cultural interest, hotels and restaurants. Black-and-yellow signs indicate the name and location of private companies and industries.

TOLLS: Tolls on Italian autostrade are quite steep, ranging from $15 to $20 for a three-hour stretch, but offering the fastest and most direct way to travel between cities. Fortunately for the agritourist, tollways are rarely necessary. However, if it suits your needs, a *Viacard*, or magnetic reusable card for tolls, is available in all tollway gas stations for 50,000 or 90,000 lire (the lines for the automatic machines taking these cards are always shortest).

FARM PRODUCE

You will be enticed by the variety of products sold at the farms such as wines, virgin olive oil, jams and honeys, cheese and salami, along with local artisans' handicrafts. U.S. customs allows U.S. residents to bring in $400 worth of foreign goods duty-free, after which a straight 10% of amount above $400 is levied. Two bottles of liquor are allowed. The import of fresh cheese or meat is strictly restricted unless it is vacuum-packed.

FINDING YOUR B&B

Directions to help you find your destination are given after each B&B description. However, they are only a small clue, as it would be impossible to find the space to give more details, and to know from which direction the traveler is arriving. The beauty of many of these B&Bs is that they are off the beaten track, but that characteristic may also make them very tricky to find. If you get lost, a common occurrence, first keep your sense of humor, then call the proprietors and/or ask locals at bars or gas stations for directions. As previously mentioned, detailed maps for the area in which you will be traveling are essential.

For reference, the 20 regions of Italy from north to south are as follows: *North*—Valle d'Aosta, Liguria, Piedmont, Friuli Veneto Giulia, Trentino Alto Adige, Lombardy, Veneto and Emilia-Romagna. *Central*—Tuscany, Umbria, The Marches, Lazio, Abruzzo and Molise. *South*—Compania, Apulia, Calabria, Basilicata, Sicily and Sardinia. Provinces indicated in addresses and on license plates are:

AL Alessandria	AN Ancona	AR Arezzo	AP Ascoli Picino
AT Asti	BA Bari	BL Belluno	BG Bergamo
BO Bologna	BZ Bolzano	BS Brescia	BR Brindisi
CZ Catanzaro	CO Como	FI Firenze	FO Forli
GE Genova	GO Gorizia	GR Grosseto	LU Lucca
MN Mantova	MI Milano	MO Modena	NA Napoli
NO Novara	PD Padova	PR Parma	PV Pavia
PG Perugia	PS Pesaro	PI Pisa	PT Pistoia
PZ Potenza	RA Ravenna	SA Salerno	SV Savona
SI Siena	TA Taranto	TR Terni	TO Torino
TN Trento	TV Treviso	VE Venezia	VC Vercelli
VR Verona	VI Vicenza	VT Viterbo	

It is important to know that addresses in the countryside often have no specific street name. A common address consists of the farm name, sometimes a *localita* (an unincorporated area, or vicinity, frequently not found on a map) and the town name followed by the province abbreviated in parentheses. (The B&B is not necessarily in that town, but it serves as a post office reference.) The localita can also be the name of the road where the B&B is located.

GLOSSARY OF FARM NAMES

The following names for farms, seen through out this guide, vary from area to area.

azienda agricola—a general term meaning farm, not necessarily offering hospitality

borgo—a small stone-walled village, usually of medieval origins

casale, casolare—variations of farmhouse, deriving from "casa"

cascina & ca'—farm in Piedmont, Lombardy and Veneto

fattoria—typically a farm in Tuscany or Umbria

hof and maso—terms meaning house and farm in the northern mountain areas

locanda—historically a restaurant with rooms for travelers passing through on horseback

masseria—fortified farms in Apulia

podere—land surrounding a farmhouse

poggio—literally describes the farm's position on a flat hilltop

tenuta—estate

torre—tower

trattoria—a simple, family-run restaurant in cities and the countryside

villa & castello—usually former home of nobility and more elaborate in services

PLANNING YOUR TRIP

INFORMATION: Italian Government Travel Offices (ENIT) can offer general information on various regions and their cultural attractions. They cannot offer specific information on restaurants and accommodations. Offices are located in:

Chicago: Italian Government Travel Office, 500 N. Michigan Ave., Chicago, IL 60611 U.S.A; tel: (312) 644-0990, fax: (312) 644-3019

London: Italian Government Travel Office, Princes Street 1, London WIR 8AY, England, tel: (004471) 408 12 54, fax: (004471) 493 66 95

New York: Italian Government Travel Office, 630 5th Ave., Suite 1565, New York, NY 10111; USA; tel: (212) 245-4822, fax: (212) 586-9249

Montreal: Italian Government Travel Office, 1 Place Ville Marie, Suite 1914, Montreal, Quebec H3B 3M9, CANADA; tel: (514) 866-7667, fax: (514) 392-1429

London: Italian Government Travel Office, Princes Street 1, London WIR 8AY, England, tel: (004471) 408 12 54, fax: (004471) 493 66 95

Sydney and Auckland: These areas are covered by the Tokyo office—Italian Government Travel Office, Itaria Seifu Kanko Kyoku (ENIT) Lion's Building -1-1-2, Moto Akasaka Minato-Ku, Tokyo 107 JAPAN; tel: (00813) 347-82051, fax: (00813) 347-99356

PERIOD OF TRAVEL

Since agritourism accommodation is usually in permanent residences, many remain open all year, but most are only open from Easter through November. If you are traveling outside this time, however, it is worth a phone call to find out if the B&B will accommodate you anyway (at very affordable rates). The best time for agritourism is without a doubt during the spring and fall months, when nature is in its glory. You can witness the *vendemia*, or grape harvest, at the end of September, the flowers blossoming in May, or olive-oil production and truffle hunts in November and December. Southern Italy can be mild and pleasant in the winter, which might be perfect for travelers who like to feel they are the only tourists around. The vast majority of Italians vacation at the same time, during the month of August, Easter weekend and Christmas, so these time periods are best avoided, if possible.

RESPONSIBILITY

Our goal in this guide is to recommend outstanding places to stay. All of the bed and breakfasts featured have been visited and selected solely on their merits. Our judgments are made on charm, setting, cleanliness, and above all warmth of welcome. No B&B ever pays to be included. However (no matter how careful we are) sometimes we misjudge a B&B's merits, or the ownership changes, or unfortunately sometimes standards are not maintained. If you find a recommended place is not as we have indicated, please let us know, and accept our sincere apologies. The rates given are those quoted to us by the B&B. Please use these figures as a guideline and be certain to ask at the time of booking what the rates are and what they include.

SHOPPING (Tax-free)

Italy is a shopper's paradise. Not only are the stores brimming with tempting merchandise, but the displays are works of art, from the tiniest fruit market to the most chic boutique. Each region seems to specialize in something. In Venice hand blown glass and handmade lace are popular. Milan is famous for its clothing and silk. Florence is a center for leather goods and gold jewelry. Rome is a fashion hub, where you can stroll the pedestrian shopping streets and browse in some of the world's most elegant shops boasting the latest designer creations. Religious items are also plentiful in Rome, particularly near St Peter's Cathedral. Naples and the surrounding area (Capri, Ravello and Positano) offer delightful coral jewelry and also a wonderful selection of ceramics. Many areas outside the metropolitan centers are well reputed for certain handicrafts; ask your B&B host about local crafts.

For purchases over Lire 300,000 an immediate cash refund of the tax amount is offered by the Italian government. Goods must be purchased at an affiliated retail outlet with the "tax-free for tourists" sign. Ask for a receipt plus the tax-free shopping cheque receipt. At the airport go first to the customs office where they will examine the items purchased and stamp receipts, and then to the "tax-free cash refund" point after passport control.

TELEPHONES

The Italian phone company (the infamous SIP) has been an object of ridicule, a source of frustration and a subject of heated conversation since its inception; and rightfully so. Over half of the phone calls initiated are never completed. Although more modern systems are being installed, it remains one of most archaic, inefficient and costly communication systems in the developed world. To make matters at least not any worse, keep the following in mind (and be prepared to "try, try again"): To make a call within

Italy, always dial "0" before the area code; from outside Italy, the "0" is eliminated. Telephone numbers can have from 4-8 digits so don't be afraid of missing numbers.

Remember that no warning is given when the time you've paid for is about to expire (the line just goes dead), so put in plenty of change. Unused coins will be refunded. There are several types of phones (in various stages of modernization) in Italy:

Gray phones (slowly being phased out) are best for local calls. These take *gettoni,* or tokens, which are available at bars and tobacco stores for 200 lire.

Regular rotary phones in bars, restaurants and many B&Bs, which you can use *a scatti,* meaning you can pay the proprietor after the call is completed.

Bright orange pay phones which accept 500, 200 and 100-lire coins as well as *gettoni.* Bright orange pay phones as above with attached apparatus permitting insertion of a *scheda telefonica,* or reusable magnetic card worth 5,000 or 10,000 lire.

NOTE: Due to the ongoing modernization process of telephone lines, phone numbers are constantly being changed, making it sometimes very difficult to contact hotels (many times they are not listed under the hotel name). A recording (in Italian) plays for only two months indicating the new number. If your Italian is not up to par, if calling from the United States, we suggest you ask the overseas operator to contact the Italian operator for translation and assistance.

To call the United States, matters have been eased by the ongoing installation of the Country Direct System, whereby with one 200-lire coin you can reach an American operator by dialing either 172-1011 for AT&T or 172-1022 for MCI. Be patient and wait the 1-2 minutes before an operator comes through. Either a collect call or a credit-card call can then be placed. If you discover this system doesn't work from some smaller towns, dial 170 to place a collect call, or try dialing direct (from a *scatti* phone), using the international code 001 + area code + number.

Dial 113 for emergencies of all kinds—24 hour service nationwide.

Dial 116 for Automobile Club for urgent breakdown assistance on the road.

TRANSPORTATION:

A car is a must for this type of travel. Most B&Bs are inaccessible by any other means of transportation. A car gives the traveler **a** great deal of independence (public transportation is frequently on strike in Italy), plus it provides the ideal means to explore the countryside thoroughly. It is best to reserve a vehicle and pre-pay by credit card before your departure to insure the best rates possible.

We wish you the best in your travels to Italy and always welcome your comments and suggestions. *Buon Viaggio!*

Descriptions of Places to Stay

In the heart of the wine valley of Piedmont, just outside and above the town of Alba, is the stately, cream-colored villa belonging to Giuliana Giacosa and her husband—Cascina Reine's gracious hosts. Besides a lovely flower garden and above-ground pool, the large home has a terra-cotta roof, a lovely arcaded patio and a fabulous view over Alba's rooftops and the surrounding countryside. Wicker chairs with plump floral cushions invite guests to relax on the patio, where at sunset they may also enjoy a refreshing mint drink with the *simpatico* hosts while sharing the day's adventures. Accommodation is offered within the ivy-covered main house, each room finely decorated with antiques, paintings and the family's personal objects. Other newer rooms have been recently added in the wing adjoining the villa. Breakfast is served either outside on the patio overlooking the vineyards and orchards, or inside in the pristine dining room with vaulted ceilings. And there's no need to worry about finding a lunch or dinner spot here, as Alba has some of the finest restaurants in Italy. The city is also famous for its wines and annual truffle festival. *Directions:* From Alba follow signs for Altavilla and Mango. Watch for a small sign on the left before the large wrought-iron gates of the inn.

CASCINA REINE
Host: Giuliana Giacosa
Localita: Altavilla 9
Alba (CN) 12051, Italy
tel: (0173) 440112
5 rooms with private bathrooms
Lire 90,000 double B&B
Breakfast only (dinner upon request)
Open all year
Very little English spoken
Region: Piedmont

Seven km from historic Bergamo and within easy reach of beautiful Lakes Como, Iseo and Garda is the home of the region's Agriturist president, Gianantonio Ardizzone. On Gianantonio's property, adjacent to the recently constructed residence where he lives with his wife and two sons, is a sprawling 15th-century farmhouse and barn complex of the type known in Lombard as a *cascina*. Installed within the cascina are three guest apartments, each of which includes a bedroom, bathroom and kitchen. The apartments are furnished modestly but comfortably, and the ambiance within and without is decidedly rustic. The cascina could perhaps use a coat of paint, but it is nestled in pretty surroundings, looking onto the small town of Nese, and backing onto the green hills where Gianantonio keeps his well tended riding horses. No meals are served here, but a nearby trattoria adequately appeases the appetite, or you may want to do some shopping before you arrive and come ready to prepare your own meals. The Grumello offers self-sufficient, conveniently located accommodation and a good value. Your hosts next-door are exceptionally helpful and sincerely warm. *Directions:* Exit from A4 autostrada at Bergamo and follow signs for Valli Bergamasche, Valle Seriana. Exit at Alzano and follow signs for hospital; turn left for Nese and again left on Via Grumello.

CASCINA GRUMELLO
Hosts: Gianantonio Ardizzone family
Localita: Fraz. Nese
Alzano Lombardo (BG) 24022, Italy
tel: (035) 510060; fax: (035) 711020
3 apartments
Lire 20,000 per person (heating/cleaning extra)
No meals served
Credit cards: VS
Open all year
Some English spoken
Region: Lombard

Anna and Gabriele had a brilliant idea when they decided to open a small inn just outside the seaside resort of Argentario, a favorite of Romans, as it is one of the few that offers moderately priced and attractive accommodations. Only a short ride from the quaint port towns of Porto Ercole, Porto Santo Stefano, the island of Giglio, and within hailing distance of a panoramic coastal drive that rivals that of Amalfi, (plus only 1-1/2 hr's drive from Fiumicino airport), La Locanda guarantees a relaxing stay in an intimate setting. The inn's twelve air-conditioned guest rooms all include bathrooms, and are simply and newly appointed. Rooms off the garden are recommended as the others face the main Aurelia road, which is a busy one. All meals are served in the public restaurant, and are served either in the inside dining room with fireplace for the cooler months, or the glassed-in summer dining room overlooking a lush garden, providing the illusion of being deep in the countryside. The southern Tuscan cuisine based on meat and fresh fish is innovative and in keeping with the family's culinary tradition (they have another hotel/restaurant on the nearby island of Giglio). *Directions:* Take the Aurelia road north from Rome. After the turnoff for Ansedonia, turn right at the inn sign. From Florence: take superstrada to Grosseto, then Aurelia road toward Rome, turning left after Orbetello at the inn's sign.

LA LOCANDA DI ANSEDONIA
Hosts: Anna Maria Bonsanti & Gabriele Rum
Via Aurelia Sud, km 140.5
Orbetello Scalo (GR) 58016, Italy
tel: (0564) 881317; fax: (0564) 881727
12 rooms with private bathrooms
Lire 120,000 double B&B
All meals served
Credit cards: VS
Open all year
Very little English spoken
Region: Tuscany

The delightful Malvarina farm has all the ingredients for the perfect B&B: Charming country-style accommodations, excellent local cuisine, warm and congenial host family, and an ideal location. Just outside town, yet immersed in lush green vegetation at the foot of the Subasio mountains, the property is comprised of the 15th-century stone farmhouse shared by Signora Maria and her two sons, and three independent cottages (converted barn and stalls). These have been divided into bedrooms and suites with ensuite bathrooms, plus two apartments with kitchenettes for 2-4 persons. *Casa Angelo* holds several bedrooms plus a sweet breakfast room with a corner fireplace and cupboards filled with colorful *Deruta* ceramics. Great care has obviously been taken in the decor of rooms where Maria has faith that her guests will treat her family's heirloom furniture as if it was their own. The old wine cellar has been cleverly converted into a cool and spacious taverna dining room. Long wooden tables line the room where guests dine *en famille*. A collection of antique farm tools and brass pots cover walls near the enormous fireplace. As if there were not enough to do and see in this rich area of Umbria, horses are available for trekking into the scenic national park just beyond the house. Plan to stay for several days. *Directions:* Exit at Capodacqua from the Perugia-Spello rte 75. Turn right then left on Via Massera (sign Radio Subasio). Follow road up to Malvarina.

MALVARINA
Hosts: Claudio & Luciano Fabrizi
Localita: Malvarina
Assisi (PG) 06081, Italy
tel & fax: (075) 8064280
10 rooms with private bathrooms, 3 apartments
Lire 86,000 double B&B
  80,000 per person half board
3-day minimum stay
Breakfast and dinner served
Open all year
Very little English spoken
Region: Umbria

We are pleased to include the newly-opened La Fornace farmhouse, since it is situated in such a desirable touring location as Assisi. It is quite obvious that Fabrizio and Bianca, the Milanese hosts originally from this part of Umbria, had the inherited farmhouse restored with their guests comfort foremost in mind. With careful attention to detail, four comfortable apartments were fashioned within the three stone houses, each with one or two bedrooms, bathroom, fully-equipped kitchenette and eating area. Interesting decorating touches such as parts of antique iron gates hung over beds, terra-cotta and white ceramic tiles in the immaculate bathrooms, and antique armoires, give the accommodations a polished country flavor. *Le Pannocchie*, the largest of the four, includes a corner fireplace, while *Papaveri*, on the second floor looks out over the flat cornfields up to magnificent Assisi and the Subasio mountains beyond. The Cascioli family takes care of guest's needs when the owners are not in residence and assures that each room is stocked with breakfast fixings each morning. This is an excellent base from which to visit such Umbrian marvels as Perugia, Spoleto, Todi and Gubbio. A swimming pool is planned for sometime in 1994. *Directions:* From Perugia-Spoleto highway 75, exit at Ospedalicchio on rte 147, turn left for Tordibetto, follow signs to Fornace.

PODERE LA FORNACE
Hosts: Bianca & Fabrizio Feliciani
Via Ombrosa
Tordibetto di Assisi (PG) 06081, Italy
tel:(075) 8039629
4 apartments
Lire 85,000-230,000 daily per apartment
3-day minimum stay
Breakfast included w/weekly stays
Open all year
English spoken well(hosts)
Region: Umbria

Few visitors to the spiritual city of Assisi are aware that the Subasio mountains flanking it feature some of the most breathtaking scenery in the country. Nestled there is a cluster of stone houses known as Le Silve, a village which served as a haven for pilgrims traveling in the 10th Century, from the Adriatic coast to Rome. In this idyllic setting they could count on a home-cooked meal and impeccable hospitality. Carrying on this tradition, Signora Taddia has recreated an ambiance of utter tranquillity, while adding her own touch of elegance. The guest rooms are tastefully furnished with simple antiques that blend harmoniously with the preserved medieval architecture. The main house contains sixteen bedrooms with bath and panoramic views, reception and a living room with fireplace. The auxiliary house has a beamed dining room, billiard and card rooms. This B&B features many of the amenities of a luxury hotel, including swimming pool, tennis and horseback riding. *Directions:* From Assisi go in the direction of Gualdo Tadino. One passes close to and should not miss the Eremo (site of St Francis' retreat). Take the winding uphill road at the sign for Armenzano and follow it for 15 km. The hotel is after Armenzano village and is well-marked.

LE SILVE DI ARMENZANO
Hostess: Daniela Taddia
Localita: Armenzano
Assisi (PG) 06081, Italy
tel: (075) 8019000; fax: (075) 8019005
15 rooms with private bathrooms, 4 suites,
7 apartments
Lire 260,000 double B&B
 full and half board available
Credit cards: all major
Open March-November
Fluent English spoken
Region: Umbria

Situated just a few miles from the Gulf of Taranto, and strategically based between the cities of Gallipoli, Taranto and Lecce, is the villa of Giacinto Mannarini. The sprawling, whitewashed modern inn was built on the original site of the Mudonato castle. Signor Mannarini, a retired Alitalia airline executive, offers warm hospitality in ten guest rooms with private bath on the ground floor of the main house, which are reached through separate entrances off an arcaded breezeway. Spotless rooms are furnished with rustic reproductions in dark wood. The property covers a 100-acres of forest and olive groves and boasts a lovely swimming pool with changing rooms and a kitchen serving meals on the poolside patio. The fine cuisine (cited in the Veronelli restaurant guide for culinary distinction) is prepared from the freshest available produce and features homemade pastas (the local *orecchiette*, or ear pasta) and desserts. Vegetarian dishes are also available. And for those tired of bread and jam, a full American breakfast is served (eggs, cheese, cereal, etc.). Signor Giacinto is a delightful host and is quite knowledgeable on his native Apulia. *Directions:* From Taranto take route 7 through Manduria and Avetrana. Three km out of town toward Salice turn left at sign for Mudonato.

BOSCO DI MUDONATO
Host: Giacinto Mannarini
Via per Salice Casella Postale 2
Avetrana (TA) 74020, Italy
tel: (099) 8704597
10 rooms, 8 with private bathrooms
1 apartment
Lire 160,000 double B&B
* 95,000 per person half board*
2-day minimum stay
Advance reservation required
Breakfast, lunch and dinner served
Closed February
English spoken well
Region: Apulia.

Tucked away in the hills of Montalbano, 38 km from Florence, is the lovely Bacchereto farm owned by the Bencini Tesi family, which opened its doors to guests several years ago as a sideline to their wine-production business. The farm comprises several historic buildings, the main house being where the family resides and breakfast is served. At a long table with visible signs of hundreds of years of use, guests are served fresh breads, homemade jams and honey. The best rooms are in the *Palazzina* an 18th-century garden and villa with seven double rooms (three with private bath) tastefully furnished with family antiques. Well-worn terra-cotta floors and beamed ceilings add to the historic atmosphere, and the kitchen and living room are at guests' disposal. The family owns an exceptional restaurant, *La Cantina di Toia* (cited in the Veronelli guide), in town within a stone building once home to Leonardo da Vinci's grandmother! Other more modest rooms are available upstairs. Maitre d'Gennaro attends meticulously to patrons, and offers an excellent selection of wines including the estate's own chianti *Carmignano of Baccolo. Directions:* From Florence (25 km) take autostrada A1 to exit Firenze Nord/Prato. Follow signs for Poggio a Caiano, Saeno, then to Bacchereto.

FATTORIA DI BACCHERETO
Hosts: Carlo Bencini Tesi family
Via Fontemorana 179
Bacchereto Carmignano (FI) 50040, Italy
tel & fax: (055) 8717191
11 rooms, 4 with private bathrooms
3 apartments
Lire 90,000 double B&B
Trattoria on premises
Open all year
English spoken well
Region: Tuscany

Just 18 km outside the enchanting town of Lucca with its enticing shops is the lovely farmhouse of the Capparoni family. Dottor Capparoni, a renowned Roman surgeon, fondly recalls childhood vacations at his grandfather's farm and believing visitors to the area would enjoy it too, started offering accommodations in the main 16th-century grand villa. But he didn't stop there—each year he added rooms in small stone houses surrounding the villa, and eventually the family property evolved into a country inn with forty rooms, all with private bath. Despite the "evolution," the country-home ambiance has been well-preserved, and guests are made to feel at home anywhere they wander—whether in the three cozy, English-style sitting rooms, the large dining rooms, or the spectacular flower garden. A favorite treat is to unwind with a drink at sunset on the spacious terrace overlooking the hills and distant towns. Each guest room differs in size and decor, but all are decorated with antiques and are warm and inviting. The dinner menu is planned in advance and posted each morning, giving guests ample time to make special requests should they so desire. Other activities available at the villa include swimming, billiards, ping pong and horseback riding. *Directions:* From Lucca (12 km) follow signs for Ponte San Pietro, then Nozzano. Villa Casanova is well-marked just beyond Nozzano.

VILLA CASANOVA
Host: Dottor Angelo Capparoni
Balbano-Nozzano (LU) 55050, Italy
tel & fax: (0583) 548429
40 rooms with private bathrooms, 5 apartments
Lire 95,000 double B&B
* 75,000 per person half board*
Breakfast and dinner served
Open all year
Credit cards: AX
English spoken well
Region: Tuscany

In the heart of the Veneto region, south of Vicenza with its villas of Palladio and lush green countryside, lies the Castello winery and estate. The handsome 15th-century villa with its long, winding drive and arched entrance way, watches proudly over the sweet town of Barbarano Vicentino. It has been the home of the Marinoni family for the past century. The large walled courtyard with manicured Renaissance garden is bordered by the family's home, the guest house (originally farmer's quarters), and converted barn, where concerts and banquets are organized. The courtyard overlooks the family's expansive vineyards from which fine red wines are produced. The independent guest house holds four bedrooms, two bathrooms, a sitting room and kitchen (breakfast is not served) which are divided according to the size of the group, and are decorated simply and pleasantly with the Marinoni family furnishings. A special treat would be a visit to the ancient wine cellar. It's an easy drive to Padua and Venice. *Directions:* Exit from the A4 at Vicenza Sud towards Barbarano Vicentino. Follow signs to Castello (20 km).

IL CASTELLO
Hosts: Elda Marinoni family
Via Castello 6
Barbarano Vicentino (VI) 36021, Italy
tel: (0444) 886055
4 rooms sharing 2 bathrooms
Lire 60,000 double
No meals served
3-day minimum stay
Open all year
English spoken well
Region: Veneto

La Casa Sola is just as its name describes—a house standing alone on a hilltop surrounded by bucolic countryside. The proprietors, a noble Genovese family, frequent their lovely vineyard property during weekends and holidays, leaving the daily management in the capable hands of the local Regoli family. The wine-and-olive-oil producing concern has helped to provide four large guest apartments within a rose-covered stone farmhouse just down the road from the main villa. Apartment No. 3 is the loveliest. Installed on two floors, comprised of a living room with fireplace, kitchen, two bedrooms and two baths, the apartment is furnished in style with refined country antiques. Botanical prints hung with bows, eyelet curtains, fresh flowers and a bottle of wine are welcoming touches. The other apartments are smaller and simpler, but each opens onto a private garden. An inviting cypress-edged swimming pool, adjacent to the villa, overlooking the valley is open to guests. Dinners or barbecues can be arranged upon request around the illuminated pool. The Gambaro's enjoy having guests sample their own high caliber wines from the cellar. The Casa Sola requires a minimum week's stay, and provides an ideal touring base in a tranquil, romantic setting for more independent travelers. *Directions:* Exit at San Donato off the Firenze-Siena superstrada. 1 km after San Donato, turn right onto dirt road at sign for Cortine/Casa Sola, and follow for 7 km.

FATTORIA CASA SOLA
Hosts: Count Gambaro family
Localita: Cortine
Barberino Val d'Elsa (FI) 50021, Italy
tel. & fax: (055) 8075028
5 apartments
Lire 650,000-1,200,000 weekly
according to apartment size and season
Occasional dinner served upon request
Open all year
English spoken well (hosts)
Region: Tuscany

Just off the main road midway between Siena and Florence, the highlight cities of Tuscany, is the square stone farmhouse with cupola owned and operated by Gianni and Cristina, a young couple from Milan. The Paretaio is particularly appealing to visitors with a passion for horseback riding, for the energetic proprietors offer everything from basic riding lessons to dressage training, and day outings through the gorgeous surrounding countryside. With that agenda, plus 20 horses to choose from, the Paretaio is recognized as one of the top riding "ranches" in Tuscany. Next to the saddle room on the first floor is a rustic and warm living room with country antiques and comfy sofas, enhanced by a vaulted brick ceiling and worn terra-cotta floors. Upstairs, the main gathering area is the dining room which features a massive fireplace and a seemingly endless wooden table. For lunch and dinner, each guest pulls up a chair to share a savory Tuscan meal. Access to the six bedrooms is from this room, and each is stylishly decorated with touches such as dried flowers, white lace curtains and not surprisingly, equestrian prints. Although riding is the main activity here, the Paretaio is an excellent base for touring the heart of Tuscany. *Directions:* Heading south from Barberino, the Paretaio is just off the road at the second right-hand turnoff.

IL PARETAIO
Hosts: Cristina & Giovanni de Marchi
Localita: San Filippo
Barberino Val d'Elsa (FI) 50021, Italy
tel: (055) 8059218; fax: (055) 8059231
6 rooms with private bathrooms
Lire 100,000 double B&B
* 95,000 per person half board*
Open March -January
English spoken well
Region: Tuscany

Conveniently located between Siena and Florence in the heart of Chianti, yet affording a feeling of escape from the rest of the world, is La Chiara farm, dating back to 1600. Covering 45-hectares of woods, vineyards and olive groves, the busy establishment is run by several families who came to this haven from Milan and reside in the stone houses surrounding the main villa. Eleven bedrooms, five of which have private baths, are dispersed throughout the informal household, which also contains a large living room, kitchen, and dining room where the mostly farm-fresh vegetarian meals are served. The common rooms and the high-ceilinged bedrooms are very modestly furnished with worn country furniture, but are spacious and airy, offering scenic views over the serene countryside. Extra beds can be easily added to rooms, making the Chiara an ideal choice for families traveling with small children. Headed by young and extremely personable Gaia and her husband, the farm swarms with activity when groups come for special lectures and courses on art and psychology. A small swimming pool not far from the house is open to guests as are horses available for trekking. *Directions:* From Barberino take the road towards Cortine. At the fork, bear right and continue 7 km to the Chiara farm.

LA CHIARA DI PRUMIANO
Hosts: Gaia Mezzadri & family
Localita: Prumiano
Barberino Val d'Elsa (FI) 50021, Italy
tel: (055) 8075330; fax: (055) 8075678
11 rooms, 5 with private bathrooms
1 apartment
Lire 90,000 double B&B
* 70,000 per person half board*
Breakfast, lunch and dinner served
Closed January
English spoken well
Region: Tuscany

On the list of bed and breakfasts with unique locations is the Dreikirchen, situated up in the Dolomite foothills with an enchanting view over a lush green valley and distant snowcapped mountain peaks. The young and energetic Wodenegg family works diligently at running the summer-season inn and restaurant and making guests feel at home in their lovely residence. Their restaurant, serving typical local meals, receives non-guest patrons as well since it shares the site of a unique historical monument—*Le Tre Chiese*, three curious, attached miniature churches which date back to the Middle Ages. The inn is reachable by either calling to be met by jeep, or on foot. An exhilarating half-hour hike takes you up to the typical mountain-style chalet with wood balconies in front. The most charming rooms are those in the older section, entirely wood-paneled, with fluffy comforters and old-fashioned wash basins. The rambling house has several common areas for guests as well as a swimming pool. Truly an incredible spot, near Siusi Alps and Val Gardena where some of the best climbing in Europe can be found. *Directions:* Exit from the Bolzano-Brennero autostrada at Klausen and take the road to and through Barbian to Bad Dreikirchen's parking on the right (after 1 km). Call the hotel from the village and they will send a jeep to collect you.

BAD DREIKIRCHEN
Hosts: Wodenegg family
San Giacomo 6
Barbian, (BZ) 39040, Italy
tel & fax: (0471) 650055
35 rooms sharing bathrooms
Lire 40,000 double B&B
* 65,000 per person half board*
Breakfast and dinner served
Open May-September
English spoken well
Region: Trentino Alto Adige

The Pomurlo farm is home to the congenial Minghelli family and covers 370-acres of hills, woods and open fields. Its location provides an excellent base from which to tour the marvels of Umbria. A winding dirt road leads past the horse stables and riding rings to the typical stone house which contains a restaurant. Inside, the tables are covered with crisp white linen, and an antique cupboard and old farm implements on the walls enhance the rustic setting. An enticing menu featuring farm-fresh specialties tempts visitors to linger over a hearty meal. Three "country suites" are situated beneath the restaurant, each consisting of two bedrooms, bathroom and kitchenette. Comfortable and cheerful, the suites are decorated with wrought-iron beds, colorful bedspreads and typical regional country antiques. A nearby converted stall houses two adorable independent rooms looking out over the lake. Other guest rooms are found in two large hilltop homes commanding a breathtaking view of the entire valley, with its grazing herds of long-horn cattle. The main house, a 12th-century tower fortress where the inn's personable hostess Daniela resides, accommodates guests in three additional suites of rooms. Conveniently located near the Rome-Florence autostrada. *Directions:* Take the Orvieto exit off of the A1 autostrada. Follow signs for Todi NOT for Baschi. On route N448 turn right at sign for Pomurlo.

POMURLO VECCHIO
Hosts: Lazzaro Minghelli & family
Localita: Lago di Corbara
Baschi (TR) 05023, Italy
tel: (0744) 950190/950475; fax: (0744) 950500
15 rooms and suites, most with private bathrooms
Lire 70,000 per person half board
Trattoria on premises
Open all year
Some English spoken
Region: Umbria.

The Locanda, a pale-yellow and brick villa dating from 1830, sits on the border Tuscany and Umbria and serves as an excellent base from which to explore this countryside. The villa's dining room features a vaulted ceiling in toast-colored brick, a enormous fireplace, French windows opening out to the flower garden, and antiques including a cupboard adorned with the family's blue-and-white china. The upstairs quarters are reserved primarily for guests, and contain six comfortable rooms which share four baths and an inviting sitting room and library. The cozy bedrooms have mansard ceilings, armoires, lovely linens and wash basins. A suite and an additional guest room are located on the ground floor in the opposite wing, once used for drying tobacco. These accommodations, each with private bath, are decorated with antique reproductions and appear more modern. The young hostess, Palmira, is a wonderful regional cook and enjoys giving lessons free of charge to her guests. Siena is only 45 km away, and the quaint medieval and renaissance villages of Pienza, Montepulciano and Montalcino are close by. *Directions:* Exit from the Rome-Florence autostrada at Val di Chiana. Head toward Bettolle, then bear right toward Siena. Follow signs for La Bandita.

LOCANDA LA BANDITA
Hostess: Palmira Fiorini
Via Bandita 72
Bettolle (SI) 53048, Italy
tel & fax: (0577) 624649
8 rooms, 4 with private bathrooms
Lire 110,000 double B&B with private bath
  80,000 per person half board
Breakfast and dinner served
Closed November
Credit cards: VS
English spoken well
Region: Tuscany

Map: 9
between
rich

ome small bed-and-breakfast-like urban hotels for the convenience
uld like to do some metropolitan sightseeing. For some reason, the
often bypassed by visitors, despite its rich past, beautiful historic
eets and elegant shops. Mentioned in another of our guides, *Italian
ineraries*, is the splendid Hotel Corona d'Oro, whose owner, Signor
Mauro _____ s two other centrally located, smaller hotels: the Orologio and the
Commercianti. Just steps away from Bologna's main piazza and Basilica is the recently
renovated Orologio, so-called because it looks onto city hall with its clock tower. The
hotel has twenty-nine rooms on three floors, and the intimate atmosphere of a family-run
establishment. The newly remodeled guest rooms are pleasantly decorated with pretty
floral-print wallpaper, photographs of the city from the 1930s and simple reproduction
furniture. An unusual but welcome treat is the full breakfast buffet served in the dining
room. Signor Orsi's other "urban inn," the modern *Hotel Commercianti*, is scheduled for
remodeling in the near future, when an effort will be made to have the decor more
closely reflect the building's 13th-century vintage. *Directions*: Located in the heart of
the historical old city.

HOTEL OROLOGIO
Hostess: Cristina Orsi
Via IV Novembre 10
Bologna 40123, Italy
tel: (051) 231253; fax: (051) 260552
29 rooms with private bathrooms

Lire 170,000-200,000 double B&B
Breakfast only
Credit cards: all major
Open all year
English spoken well
Region: Emilia-Romagna

Just off the busy road that connects the major towns of Umbria—Perugia, Assisi, Spoleto, and Todi—is the elegant country house Giulia, which has been in the Petrucci family since its 14th-century origins. Later additions were built on to the stone villa, one of which Signora Caterina has opened up to guests. Time seems to have stood still in the six bedrooms, all but one with ensuite bathroom, and filled with grandmother Giulia's lovely antique iron-wrought beds, armoires, and period paintings. They are divided between three floors, accessed by a steep stone staircase, the largest having a ceiling fresco depicting the local landscape. Breakfast is served either in the chandeliered dining room upstairs, with oriental carpets, lace curtains, and large fireplace, or under the oak trees in the front garden during the warmer months. Part of the barn has been recently converted into two independent units which include a fully-equipped kitchenette for up to 4 persons. Although the large swimming pool overlooks a rather barren field and the distant main road, it is a welcome respite after a full day of touring, which guests will be doing a lot of from this strategically convenient location. *Directions:* Just off the Perugia-Spoleto rte. 75 between Trevi and Campello.

CASA GIULIA
Hostess: Caterina Alessandrini Petrucci
Via SS Flaminia km.140.1
Bovara di Trevi (PG) 06039, Italy
tel: (0742) 78257
6 rooms, 5 with private bathrooms
Lire 140,000 double B&B
Breakfast only
Open all year
Some English spoken
Region: Umbria

Brisighella is a gem. The town comes to life during the months of June and July when it celebrates its annual Medieval Festival. Games of the period are re-enacted, and medieval music, literature and dance are produced. Locals attire themselves in appropriate costume and the village's narrow streets are illuminated nightly by torches for the occasion. Just out of town, past the thermal hot springs is the sweet home of a young Milanese couple, Ettore and Adriana, who moved here recently, taking over the vineyards and orchards of the 10-hectare property. Guests are treated to the host's excellent Sangiovese and Chardonnay wines. They have renovated the barn next to their small stone house, creating three guest rooms as well as a rustic dining area with exposed beams and a large fireplace where guests gather for typical Romagna-style meals. Rooms are decorated with simple country furnishings. The atmosphere is casual and the value excellent. While in the vicinity don't miss the mosaics in Ravenna, the historical center of Bologna and the international ceramic museum in Faenza. *Directions:* Take Faenza exit from the A14 between Bologna and Rimini. Follow signs for Brisighella. At town take left turn for Terme/Modigliona. Il Palazzo is the third house on the left after the Hotel Terme.

IL PALAZZO
Hosts: Ettore Matarese family
Via Baccagnano 11
Brisighella (RA) 48013, Italy
tel: (0546) 80338
3 rooms, 2 with private bathrooms
Lire 70,000 double B&B
* 60,000 per person half board*
3-day minimum stay or 20% surcharge
Breakfast, lunch and dinner served
Open all year
English spoken well
Region: Emilia-Romagna

For those who have a passion for horseback riding, or with an urge to learn, La Mandria provides the opportunity to do either while on holiday. As host and horseman Davide Felice Aondio proudly explains, his horse farm has been in existence for over 30 years and has been a model for riding resorts. Situated near the foothills of the Alps and between the cities of Turin and Milan, the vast, flat property borders a 5,000-hectare national park, offering spectacular scenery and endless possibilities for horseback excursions. The complex is made up of horse stables, haylofts, guest rooms, dining room and the private homes of the proprietor and his son, Marco's, family. The whole forms a square with riding rings in the center. As a national equestrian training center, lessons of every nature are offered for all ages. Six very basic bedrooms with bath are reserved for guests, and good local fare is served in the rustic dining room. Golf, swimming and tennis facilities are available nearby. Two side trips that must not be missed are first, to spellbinding Lake Maggiore, and then to the intriguing medieval town of Ricetto where the houses and streets are made of smooth stones. *Directions:* Take Carisio exit from the Milan-Turin autostrada. Head toward Biella, but at town of Candelo turn right for Mottalciata. Mandria is on the right.

LA MANDRIA
Hosts: Marco Aondio family
Candelo (VC) 13062, Italy
tel: (015) 2536078
6 rooms with private bathrooms
Lire 140,000 double B&B
* 115,000 per person half board*
Breakfast, lunch and dinner served
Open all year
English spoken well
Region: Piedmont

Poetically named after a classic Italian tale by Cesare Pavese, a native of this area, the *Luna e i Falo* (meaning the moon and the fire) farmhouse was lovingly restored by Turin couple Ester and Franco Carnero. The ritual described in the story is still performed on the eighth of August every year when local farmers collect old grapevines and burn them under the full moon in hopes of a good crop. On that night, the bonfires dotting hills surrounding the farm create quite a spectacle. The Carnero's brick home has arched windows and an arcaded front terrace, with two double rooms and one suite which they have made available to visitors. For a country home, the spacious living/dining area is elaborately furnished with Renaissance period pieces. The bedrooms reveal a combination of old and new decor and sweeping views of the countryside, known for its wineries. The emphasis at the Luna e i Falo is on the cuisine, and logically so. The proprietors previously owned a highly regarded restaurant in Turin, and they did not leave their culinary skills behind. They continue to practice them, producing excellent handmade pasta (no machines in Ester's kitchen!), among other delicacies. *Directions:* From Asti follow the signs for Canelli and, before town, take a right up the hill to Castello. The farmhouse is on the right side.

LA LUNA E I FALO
Hosts: Ester & Franco Carnero
Localita Aie 37, Canelli (AT) 14053, Italy
tel: (0141) 831643
2 rooms with private bathrooms
1 apartment for 4 persons
Lire 120,000 double B&B
* 90,000 per person half board*
2-day minimum stay
Breakfast and dinner served
Open all year
No English spoken (French)
Region: Piedmont

North of Florence between Prato and Pistoia is a pocket of little-known, yet entrancing countryside comprising the Calvana Mountains and Bisenzio Valley. Grazia, Mario and their three children have lived there all their lives and love sharing their enthusiasm for the area through offering accommodation to visitors. Although the entrance and exterior leave a little to be desired in terms of aesthetics, the property is beautifully situated overlooking a wooded valley and private lake out in the back. What really counts here is the hosts' warmth and their sincere effort to make their guests feel at home. The six bedrooms with accompanying immaculate baths are sweet and simple, decorated with comfortable, old-fashioned furniture. Guests convene downstairs for breakfast and dinner in the rustic dining room with exposed beams and fireplace. Off the dining room is the kitchen, where you can watch Grazia rolling out fresh pasta. From lasagna and tortelli to polenta and desserts, Grazia's culinary arts reflect the influence of the bordering regions of Tuscany and Emilia. A visit to the welcoming Ponte alla Villa offers an opportunity to familiarize yourself with the customs of an area off the beaten track. *Directions:* From Prato, take route 325 north to Vernio, then bear left toward Cantagallo. Watch for signs for the B&B at Luicciana.

PONTE ALLA VILLA
Hosts: Grazia Gori & Mario Michelagnoli
Localita: Luicciana 273-La Villa
Cantagallo (FI) 50040, Italy
tel: (0574) 956094 / 956244
8 rooms with private bathrooms
Lire 60,000 double B&B
 45,000 per person half board
2-day minimum stay
Breakfast lunch and dinner served
Open all year—weekends only during winter
Very little English spoken
Region: Tuscany

La Minerva is located in a quiet section of Capri, slightly off the beaten track, yet still quite central, permitting easy access to the more bustling areas of town—a walker's paradise with no motorized transportation allowed. The street-level entrance is the hotel's third-floor living room, a vast chamber with stark-white tiled floors and ground-to-ceiling windows overlooking the sea. This captivating view will strike you every time you come and go, or eat breakfast, as the same panorama greets you in the dining room. The rest of the small hotel is beneath, with the reception and breakfast area on the ground floor. Signora Esposito has decorated the eighteen rooms sweetly and simply with colorful tiled floors and scattered antiques. Each bedroom has a private balcony overlooking umbrella-pine woods and the sea. All rooms also have their own bath, done in blue and white tile. The family lives in one section of the building, but share with guests their homey living room, with family photos and lace doilies on the tables. This is a peaceful spot to get away, but not too far away. *Directions:* It's best to stop by the tourist office as you get off the ferry and get a map of Capri, showing the Via Occhio Marino.

LA MINERVA
Hosts: Luigi Esposito family
Via Occhio Marino 8
Capri (NA) 80073, Italy
tel & fax: (081) 8377067
18 rooms with private bathrooms
Lire 190,000 double B&B
Breakfast only
Credit cards: VS,MC
Open Easter-October
Some English spoken
Region: Campania

The Villa Krupp is a delightful small hotel whose claim to local fame can be found in its guest book, boasting such illustrious names as Lenin and Gorky. Signor Coppola, the cordial and proud proprietor, took over the property in 1964. The charming hotel contains twelve bedrooms, each with its own bath, in a somewhat modern and boxy building alongside the host's own residence. The Krupp is dramatically situated in one of the most beautiful corners of Capri's Augusto Park, atop a steep, sheer cliff dropping to the sparkling turquoise sea beneath. The site overlooks the Faraglioni rock formation (a symbol of the island) and Marina Piccola, one of Capri's two ports. A thousand steps lead from its top edge down to the seaside. The Villa Krupp has its own set of steps leading up to the best vantage point from which to admire this spectacular panorama. The light-filled guest rooms, each featuring its own terrace and bath, are decorated with simple antiques and tiled with the brightly colored ceramics typical of Capri. Room No. 18 is a particular favorite due to its relatively large sea view terrace. Breakfast is served on the veranda or outside on the flowered terrace. *Directions:* Take the cable car up to Capri, walk through the main square, then down the Via Emanuele to Matteotti (on the right).

VILLA KRUPP
Hosts: Coppola family
Viale Matteotti 12
Capri (NA) 80073, Italy
tel: (081) 8370362; fax: (081) 8376489
12 rooms with private bathrooms
Lire 150,000-180,000 double B&B
Breakfast only
Open all year
Some English spoken
Region: Campania

Capri has long had a reputation for being an exclusive island. Charging prices substantially higher than the rest of the country, only the elite were able to afford to vacation there. However, times have changed and the cost of tourism across Italy has soared, bringing other destinations more in line with Capri in terms of expense, therefore making it relatively more affordable than it once was. Unfortunately, agritourism does not exist on the island, but there are several small, family-run hotels that provide a bed and breakfast "feeling." One such establishment belongs to Antonino Vuotto and his wife, a local couple who have opened up their centrally located prim white home in the town of Capri, making four bedrooms available to guests. The rooms are very clean and neat, with typically tiled floors, and private baths and balconies in each. Some even have a view of the sea. Breakfast is brought to your room (there is no common dining room), and is the only meal served, but the Villa's convenient location makes it easy to get to any of Capri's fine restaurants for lunch and dinner. *Directions:* Take the cable car up to Capri. Go through the main town square to Via Emanuele, past the Quisisana Hotel and continue to the end of the street. Turn left onto Via Certosa, then left again on Cerio. The Villa is on the corner and is not marked with a sign.

VILLA VUOTTO
Hosts: Antonino Vuotto family
Via Campo di Teste 2
Capri (NA) 80073, Italy
tel: (081) 8370230
4 rooms with private bathrooms
Lire 110,000 double B&B
Breakfast only
Open all year
Very little English spoken
Region: Campania

The Ombria farmhouse nestles amidst the foothills just 30 km from both beautifully austere Bergamo and Lecco on Lake Como. Meticulous restoration of the stone house dating from 1613 started over four years ago and the B&B activity finally began last year. Cordial host, Luciano, has given great attention to detail and to preserving the original architectural features (such as the faithful reproduction of the original stone floor patterns). An arched entryway leads into a stone courtyard with gazebo and open grill, where tables are set for summertime meals. The Ombria has already made a name for itself with its exceptional restaurant where patrons enjoy candlelit international cuisine in the intimate stone-walled dining room—as long as they make reservations three months in advance! Luciano retired early to realize his dream of running a country inn and breeding French and Swiss goats for cheese production. The three doubles and one suite available are decorated with fine antiques and wrought-iron beds. Original fireplaces, exposed beams, warm wood floors, stone walls and a common cozy sitting room make them particularly appealing. A special place at a very special price. *Directions:* From Milan take the A4 autostrada, exit at Agrate and head north toward Lecco on Route 36. At route 342 turn right toward Caprino Bergamasco and follow signs for Ombria. 15 km from Bergamo.

OMBRIA
Host: Luciano Marchesin
Localita: Celana
Caprino Bergamasco
(BG) 24030, Italy
tel: (035) 781668
3 rooms and 1 suite with private bathrooms
Lire 50,000 per person half board
Breakfast and dinner served
Open all year
English spoken well
Region: Lombardy

West of Chianti, just behind the medieval hilltop village of Casole d'Elsa, and half an hour from the picturesque towns of Siena and San Gimignano, is a typical Tuscan stone farmhouse. It is this place that the seven-member Zito family has called home for the past nine years, ever since they made the unanimous and courageous decision to uproot from New York and start over in Italy, blending almost seamlessly into the culture and tranquil lifestyle of their country of origin. Together they took on the project of restoring the house, landscaping, and furnishing the seven guest rooms on the second floor above their living quarters. The bedrooms, each with spotless blue-and-white-tiled bathrooms and welcoming flowers, retain a simple country flavor, enhanced by the worn terra-cotta brick floors, beamed ceilings, antique armoires and bedside tables, and wrought-iron beds. Restoration work on the barn has just been completed, offering a lovely 2-bedroom house for weekly stays. Breakfast consisting of fresh-baked cakes and breads is served until noon outside on the rose-covered stone patio overlooking the hillsides and herds of sheep. Judging by the appreciative comments in the guest book, it is evident that Alfred and Rose have offered much happiness to many travelers. *Directions:* From Florence take the superstrada toward Siena, exiting at Colle Val d'Elsa. Take Route 68 and turn left for Casole d'Elsa. The inn is just outside town beyond the Hotel Pietralta.

PODERE CAPRETTO
Hosts: Alfred & Rose Zito
Casole d'Elsa (SI) 53031, Italy
tel: (0577) 948550
7 rooms with private bathrooms
1 apartment
Lire 98,000 double B&B
Breakfast only
Open all year
Fluent English spoken
Region: Tuscany

What a pleasant surprise to discover the Solarola, a sunny yellow villa as its name implies, in the flat Midwestern-like countryside around Bologna. It is, in a word "perfect." Gracious hosts Antonella and Valentino (a renowned architect), took over the family farm several years ago, transforming one of its two turn-of-the-century villas into a private home and the other into a guest house with five double rooms, as well as a restaurant, living room, billiard room and outdoor gazebo and beautiful swimming pool. Antonella decorated the guest villa to be romantic and refined, yet warm and inviting, without a single detail overlooked. Each room is named after a flower and everything from wallpaper, botanical prints and fluffy comforters to motifs on lamp shades and bed frames, bouquets and even room fragrance conform to the floral theme in color and appearance. The hosts' passion for the Victorian period is apparent in details such as cupboards filled with china, lace curtains and doilies, dried-flower bouquets, old family photos and Tiffany lamps. In addition, Antonella has been rightfully praised in several publications for her refined cuisine, creating inventive combinations with the freshest of ingredients to the delight of guests. A first-rate splurge. *Directions:* Exit from autostrada A14 at Castel S. Pietro and turn right towards Medicina for 5 km. Turn right at Via S.Paolo and follow to end then right again on Via S.Croce to Solarola.

LOCANDA SOLAROLA
Hosts: Antonella Scardovi & Valentino Parmiani
Via San Croce 5
Castel Guelfo (BO) 40023, Italy
tel: (0542) 670102 / 670089; fax:(0542) 670222
5 doubles with private bathrooms
Lire 240,000 double B&B
Breakfast lunch and dinner served
Credit cards: VS
Open all year
Some English spoken
Region: Emilia-Romagna

The Villa Gaidello farm has been written up on several occasions (in *Bon Appetit*, *Cuisine*, *Eating in Italy*), mostly as a result of its superb cuisine. There is nothing extravagant about hostess Paola Bini's recipes, carefully prepared by local women. Rather, the secret to her success seems to lie in the revival of basic traditional dishes using the freshest possible ingredients. Pasta is made daily (a great treat to watch) and features all the local variations on tagliatelle, pappardelle and stricchettoni. Reservations for dinner must be made several days in advance. Paola was one of the pioneers in agriturismo, transforming her grandmother's nearly 200-year-old farmhouse into a guest house and restaurant 20 years ago. One to five guests are accommodated in each of the three suites, which include kitchen and sitting room. The suites are cozy and rustic with exposed-brick walls, country antiques and lace curtains. The dining room, set with doilies and ceramic, is situated in the converted hayloft and overlooks the vast garden and a small pond. The Gaidello provides a convenient stopover just off the Bologna-Milan autostrada. *Directions:* Exit the autostrada at Castelfranco, Modena Sud. Follow Via Emilia/Route 9, turning left at the sign for Gaidello.

VILLA GAIDELLO
Hostess: Paola Bini
Via Gaidello 18
Castelfranco Emilia (MO) 41013, Italy
tel: (059) 926806; fax: (059) 926620
3 suites with private bathrooms
Lire 154,000 double B&B
Breakfast lunch and dinner served
Closed August, Restaurant closed Sundays
Very little English spoken
Region: Emilia-Romagna

The Podere San Quirico is a sweet little Tuscan farmhouse with an even sweeter owner and hostess, Maria Consiglio Picone, a former theater costume designer who moved to Tuscany from her native Naples 22 years ago. Her B&B activity commenced soon afterward, once the 14th-century crumbling stone farmhouse had been lovingly pieced back together. Maria proudly points out how the original exposed-beam structure dating from 1300 has been kept intact, and how her enchanting garden has developed over the years. Six guest rooms in her home are decorated in harmony with the house, containing very simple country furniture and wrought-iron beds. Most rooms have their own spotless bath, as well as a gorgeous view over the soft green countryside. The former horse stalls have been converted into a dining room and kitchen for convenience of visitors. For weekly stays, a separate two-bedroom house is also available. Just half an hour from Siena (a must-see destination in this vicinity), and at the foot of the Chianti region, the San Quirico serves as an ideal touring base. *Directions:* Depending on the direction of your approach, exit either at Monte San Savino or Valdarno off the A1 Firenze-Roma highway. Follow signs for Castelnuovo Berardenga. The B&B is just outside town and well-marked.

PODERE SAN QUIRICO
Hostess: Maria Consiglio Picone
Via del Paradiso 1
Castelnuovo Berardenga (SI) 53019, Italy
tel & fax: (0577) 355206
6 rooms, 4 with private bathrooms
1 apartment
Lire 85,000 double only
Breakfast served upon request
Open all year
Some English spoken
Region: Tuscany

To the west of Cortina, the most fashionable ski area in the Dolomites, is Val Gardena, which is almost too storybook-perfect to be true. The valley, once part of Austria, still preserves its Germanic heritage, evident in the language, cuisine and culture. It has always been a favorite vacation spot for Italians, offering good value not only in the winter, but during the hot month of August, when visitors can take hikes in the cool woods and sleep well at night under a comforter. The Gshtroffhof, owned by the warmhearted Rier family, is right in the heart of the valley, on the road leading up to the Alps of Siusi. Dating back to 1500, it is a typical white chalet with wood trim and shutters, with windowsills and balconies overflowing with cascading geraniums of all colors. The four guest rooms are simple and cozy, as is the rest of the house, and share nearby bathrooms. Decorated modestly with light pinewood furniture, each has a balcony affording splendid views over the green valley, snowcapped peaks and the quaint town of Siusi below. As with most farm families here, the Rier's main livelihood is raising cows, whose bells produce the only sound breaking the tranquillity of the valley. *Directions:* From the Verona-Brennero autostrada, take exit Bolzano Nord and follow signs for Siusi. After town, well before Castelrotto, turn right for Alps, then left at the sign for Gschtroffhof.

GSCHTROFFHOF
Hosts: Hermann Rier family
San Valentino 36
Castelrotto (BZ) 39040, Italy
tel: (0471) 706525
4 rooms sharing bathrooms
Lire 44,000 double B&B
Breakfast only
Open all year
No English spoken (German)
Region: Alto Adige

Rier is a common family name in the Val Gardena area, and though they are neighbors, the Rier family who own the Marmsolerhof, are not related to the proprietors of the Gschtrtoffhof. This adorable bed and breakfast is owned and run by a young local couple with four children. The crisp white house with its old stone-and-wood attached barn has been in the same family for over 400 years was been recently renovated, giving the property a fresh new look. The entrance foyer walls are adorned with antique farm tools, harnesses and cow bells. On the same floor is a dining room with individual tables where guests can enjoy breakfast with a view overlooking the velvet green hillside. The five guest rooms, all but one with private bath, are simply and comfortably furnished with pinewood beds and armoires, bright-orange curtains and fluffy comforters. Stepping out on the balcony reveals a breathtaking panorama of the pine-covered mountains. The Riers are happy to suggest scenic places to explore by car or on foot, and know the best places for rock climbing up into one of the most spectacular ranges in Europe. *Directions:* Exit at Bolzano Nord from the Verona-Brennero autostrada and follow signs for Siusi. Beyond town, before Castelrotto, turn right for Alps, then left for Marmsolerhof.

MARMSOLERHOF
Hosts: August Rier family
San Valentino 35
Castelrotto (BZ) 39040, Italy
tel: (0471) 706514
5 rooms, 4 with private bathrooms
Lire 52,000 double B&B
Breakfast only
Open all year
Very little English spoken (German)
Region: Alto Adige

Tucked away off a winding mountain road in the enchanting Siusi Alps is a typical Tyrolian farmhouse, called *mas* in this northern region of Alto Adige. The Jaider family has resided here ever since the 15th Century, traditionally maintaining a dairy farm. Their inviting home is colorfully accented with green shutters and flower-laden boxes at every window. Two wooden barns are connected to the residence via a stone terrace. Signora Jaider runs her home with the hotel efficiency which has come to be expected by visitors to this predominantly German-speaking area, once belonging to Austria. Meals are served out on the terrace in clement weather, or in the original dining room, whose charm is enhanced by the low, wood-paneled ceiling (so constructed to retain heat) with its hand painted edelweiss flowers. Cuisine in this region reflects its Austrian heritage, with *speck* ham, meat and potatoes, and apple strudel winning over pasta dishes. Lovely country antiques are dispersed throughout the house and the eight bedrooms, which are wood-paneled from floor to ceiling and have pretty valley views. Two guest rooms include balconies. *Directions:* Exit at Bolzano Nord from autostrada A22, following signs for Fie and Alpe di Siusi. Pass through Siusi and turn off to the left for Tisana. San Osvaldo is on the left after Tisana.

TSCHOTSCHERHOF
Hosts: Jaider family
San Osvaldo 19
Castelrotto (BZ) 39040, Italy
tel: (0471) 706013
8 rooms with private bathrooms
Lire 56,000 double B&B
  42,000 per person half board
All meals served
Open March-October
Very little English spoken (German)
Region: Alto Adige

Liguria is the sliver of a region touching France and boasting the Italian Riviera, including such celebrated port towns as Portofino, Santa Margherita, San Remo and Cinque Terre. Agriturismo is something new for the Ligurians; and tourism has always drifted seaward. From the busy coastal town of Sestri Levante, a 6 km winding road leads up a mountain to the rather remote Monte Pu farm, where a group of people from Milan migrated in search of a simpler and saner way of life. For serenity, they could hardly have chosen a more ideal or isolated spot. The three-story, peach-color brick farmhouse complex, dating from 1400, commands a marvelous sweeping view over wooded mountains and valleys down to the sea, 700 feet below. The seven guest rooms (with three baths close by), are simple and immaculate, with light pine furniture and wildflower bouquets. Downstairs is the warm and airy dining room where a full country breakfast awaits guests each morning. Dinner is prepared by a young couple and served outside in the courtyard in warmer months. The culinary emphasis is on vegetarian dishes such as risotto, soups and salads, prepared with ingredients straight from the garden. Horses are available for riding in the forest preserves surrounding the property. *Directions:* Exit from the Genova-Livorno autostrada at Sestri Levante and follow signs for Casarza Ligure, Castiglione, and then Campegli to Monte Pu.

MONTE PU
Hostess: Aurora Giani
Castiglione Chiavarese (GE) 16030, Italy
tel & fax: (0185) 408.027 / 408441
7 rooms, 2 with private bathrooms
1 apartment
Lire 120,000 double B&B
All meals served
Open Easter-December
English spoken well
Region: Liguria

On a hilltop in Pomino wine country sits the 15th-century Medici villa that belongs to the Nicolodi family, only its third proprietors. Surrounded by hundreds of acres of scenic vineyards, olive groves and cypress woods, the large ivy-covered villa also features a renaissance garden with stone statuary. Within the historic villa are six comfortable guest rooms, only one with private bath. Six independent apartments have recently been added in the farmhouses which dot the vast property. The home is steeped in the past. With its elaborate, worn antiques, gilt mirrors, period paintings, oriental carpets, chandeliers, and enormous gray-stone fireplaces, the place seems frozen in time. Yet a casual and welcoming atmosphere is sensed immediately. And this is how the Nicolodis like it. They put on no false airs and guests may wander about freely. Their home is virtually your home. Signora is Neopolitan, as her cooking confirms, and Signor, who has traveled widely and spent a long period in Africa, sincerely enjoy receiving guests at home. With facilities for tennis, swimming, and billiards, a jacuzzi, beautiful scenery and excellent meals (including full American-style breakfast), they do a good job of persuading them to stay. *Directions:* From Florence follow signs for Pontassieve. After Rufina, turn right for Pomina.

LA SOSTA AI BUSINI
Hosts: Marcello Nicolodi family
Localita Castiglioni di Rufina
Via Scopeti 28, Rufina (FI) 50068, Italy
tel: (055) 8397809; fax: (055) 8397004
6 rooms, 1 with private bathroom, 6 apartments
Lire 140,000 double B&B
* 100,000 per person half board*
2-day minimum stay
Breakfast lunch and dinner served
Open Easter-January 15
English spoken well
Credit cards: VS, DC
Region: Tuscany

We were delighted to hear that one of our favorite B&B hostesses, the delightful Stella Casolaro, has just started another B&B in her new home after having sold the Scuderia in Badia di Passignano. If you were ever one of her fortunate guests you would understand why travelers come back and stay with her year after year. Her new location, 35 km west of Siena, is in the lesser-known, more rugged part of the Tuscan countryside. In fact, much to the delight of husband, Carlo, who has a passion for hunting for porcini mushrooms, dense woods cover the entire area. The white 60-year-old house with circling garden is right on the edge of the quaint village of Ciciano. Three sweet bedrooms, each with its own bathroom, and a living room have been reserved for guests on the couple's second floor, while they reside on the third floor. All rooms have a double wrought-iron bed with a variety of country antiques in keeping with the simple yet homey ambiance. Guests are treated to a special breakfast including freshly-baked cakes. It's like "coming home." Directions: From Siena, take rte. 73 towards Grosseto. After Frosini, turn off to the right for Chiusdino, then Ciciano.

CASA ITALIA
Hosts: Stella & Carlo Casolaro
Via Massetana 5
Ciciano-Chiusdino (SI) 53010, Italy
tel: (0577) 750656; fax: (055) 7321137
3 rooms with private bathrooms, 3 apartments.
Lire 80,000 double B&B
  500,000-800,000 weekly for apartments
Breakfast only (dinner upon request)
Open all year
No English spoken
Region: Tuscany

It would be difficult to find another expatriate as enthusiastic about Italy as is English B&B owner, Sarah Townsend. She and husband Johnny have poured their heart and soul into making Il Bacchino a veritable cultural, epicurean and visual feast. A mere ten minute walk from the fine antique center of Cortona, this small but beautiful 17th-century villa has been lovingly restored to its former glory. The original interior with its wood beams, vaulted ceilings, and stone floors is filled with elegant period antiques and paintings. Sarah's open house philosophy allows guests to lounge in any of the three cozy sitting rooms or outside on the wicker sofas overlooking her marvelous terraced 17th-century Italian garden—just another one of her many talents. A spectacular mosaic swimming pool is perched on the upper terrace surrounded by breathtaking countryside views. Four sweetly decorated bedrooms are reserved for guests on the second floor along with an inviting living room displaying trompe l'oeil designs by Sarah. A lovely sideboard filled with a collection of blue and white china, dominates the dining room where guests are treated to Sarah's innovative meals. Their former farmhouse 10 minutes away, is available for weekly rentals. Simply delightful. Directions: It is best to call when you reach the center of Cortona.

IL BACCHINO
Hosts: Sarah & Johnny Townsend
Torreone 126
Cortona (AR) 52044, Italy
tel & fax: (0575) 603284
Four rooms, 3 with private bathrooms
Lire 180,000 (approximate) double B&B
2-day minimum stay
Breakfast and dinner served
Open April-November
Fluent English spoken
Region: Tuscany

Picturesque Courmayeur, on the Italian side of the tunnel cutting through Mont Blanc into France, is a popular ski and summer resort. In the summer months comfortable temperatures and spectacular mountain scenery along with activities as hiking, golf, horseback riding and kayaking attract many visitors. The warm Berthod family have been offering hospitality to guests for some time, greeting them by name as they return "home" year after year. The old stone chalet and barn, squeezed between other houses in the center of the centuries-old village, Entreves, outside Courmayeur, has been recently restored using old and new materials. The cozy reception area maintains its original rustic flavor with flagstone floors and beams, hanging brass pots, typical locally-made pine furniture, and homey touches as dried flower arrangements and lace curtains. The 23 simply appointed rooms have been divided between two buildings and offer amenities of a standard hotel. A hearty breakfast is the only meal served, however half board arrangements can be obtained for longer stays with local restaurants. La Grange is an efficiently-run B&B right at the foot of the snow-capped Alps. Directions: From Aosta where autostrada A5 ends, continue on rte. 26 to Courmayeur. Entreves is 5 km beyond.

LA GRANGE
Hosts: Berthod Family
Fraz. Entreves
Courmayeur (AO) 11013, Italy
tel: (0165) 89274; fax: (0165) 89316
23 rooms with private bathrooms
Lire 140,000 double B&B (high season)
Breakfast only
Credit Cards: AX, VS
Closed: May, June, October, November
English spoken well
Region: Val d'Aosta

La Mongolfiera is one of the handful of luxurious B&Bs included in this guide. Located in the Franciacorta wine region just south of Lake Iseo between the major cities of Bergamo and Brescia, this ivy-covered guest house is part of the vast Bellavista wine estate owned by Signor Vittorio Moretti. Perched idyllically on a hilltop overlooking a valley carpeted with grape vines, the small inn has six elegant bedrooms with private bath, telephone, TV and minibar. Original decorations such as colorful ceramic tile interspersed in the terra-cotta floors, hand painted nature motifs (birds, butterflies, fruit, flowers), and tapestry bedspreads coordinate perfectly with the fine antique furniture. Four rooms have their own terrace, and the "Sunflower" room is a suite with an extra bed in the loft. Guests have full access to the house, whose spacious downstairs includes a living room, a splendid country-style dining room with fruit garlands painted between the windows, a card room with grand piano, and an outdoor patio filled with overflowing flowerpots where dinner is served, weather permitting. This idyllic spot has just been honored a place in the Michelin guide. Directions: Take the Rovato exit from the Milan-Venice A4 highway. Head toward Erbusco, turning right at the main square in town, then follow signs to Mongolfiera/Bellavista.

LA MONGOLFIERA
Host: Vittorio Moretti
Director: Bruno Bosio
Localita: Bellavista
Erbusco (BS) 25030, Italy
tel: (030) 7760220; fax: (030) 7760386
5 rooms with private bathrooms, 1 suite
Lire 190,000 double B&B (3-day minimum)
All meals served
Credit cards: all major
Open all year
English spoken well
Region: Lombardia

For travelers who want to explore another facet of Italy's many-sided culture, the southern-most, "heel-side" of the boot-shaped peninsula, known as *Puglia*, merits investigation. It is a land with spectacular coastlines, villages with distinct Greek and Turkish influence, endless lines of olive groves, fields of wild flowers, and a rich history of art including Pugliese Romanesque and Baroque (Bari's Santa Nicola church is simply one of the most beautiful in Italy). All of this plus exquisite cuisine and a warm and open people await in *Puglia*, (Apulia) as does the Masseria Salamina, a 16th-century fortified farmhouse located between Bari and Brindisi. The driveway leads us to the sand-colored castle with turreted tower with expansive vistas sweeping to the sea. The farm covers hundred acres of land and produces primarily olive oil. Through the courtyard are found the seven suites, each with a separate entrance and freshly decorated with reproductions and wicker furniture. Host Gianvincenzo and family live in the main wing and run their masseria with hotel efficiency and service. A large lofty restaurant with terra-cotta floors provides all meals for guests. Eight additional apartments are now available for longer stays. Directions: From the SS16 exit at Fasano. Follow signs for Pezze di Greco, and take the second right in town.

MASSERIA SALAMINA
Host: Gianvincenzo De Miccolis Angelini
Localita: Pezze di Greco
Fasano (BR) 70121, Italy
tel & fax: (080) 727307 / 728582
7 suites with private bathrooms, 8 apartments
Lire 90,000-200,000 double B&B
* 75,000-135,000 per person half board*
1 week minimum stay in July & August
All meals served
Open all year
Some English spoken
Region: Apulia

Simona and Luciano Nenna chose an idyllic location in which to relocate, surrounding themselves with hundreds of acres of woods, rivers, valleys and best of all, utter tranquillity. Ten years ago, this ambitious and hospitable couple began restoring an isolated village made up of 12 stone houses, transforming it into a rustic retreat for their exhausted friends from Rome. Besides producing all their own fruits and vegetables, their main activity is equestrian. They have 20 horses, well-equipped stables, indoor and outdoor rings, riding school and organized excursions into the scenic countryside. The Noci house contains seven simple rooms with bath, which retain their original terra-cotta floors and wood-beamed ceilings, and are decorated with country furniture. La Terrazza, originally a hunting lodge, houses nine guestrooms with bath, including its namesake terrace room. Other buildings are La Quercia, the dining hall where guests share hearty Umbrian specialties, accompanied by Orvieto wines at long tables, and the bar with huge fireplace and occasional live entertainment. Alternative activities include on-site tennis and swimming. Directions: Exit at Fabro from Rome-Firenze A1 autostrada. Follow signs for Parrano, (7 km) turning right at Casella sign and continue for another 7 km on a rough gravel road.

LA CASELLA
Hosts: Simona & Luciano Nenna
Ficulle (TR) 05016, Italy
tel: (0763) 86075; fax: (0763) 86684
28 rooms with private bathrooms
Lire 96,000 double B&B
 90,000 per person half board
Breakfast and dinner served
Credit cards: all major
Closed January
Fluent English spoken
Region: Umbria

Given the unbearable August heat in most parts of the country, and the inevitably overcrowded conditions at the seaside resorts during that month, it is small wonder that the cooler elevations of the Alps and Dolomites have become a favorite vacation destinations for Italian families. In addition to offering the ideal atmosphere for relaxation and recharging, it offers invigorating fresh mountain air, numerous outdoor activities, spectacular scenery and best of all, the least expensive "getaway" available in the country. The darling Merlhof bed and breakfast is owned and operated by the Kompatschers, who have created seven guestrooms within their family home in the town of Fie. The traditional, Tyrolian-style white-and dark-wood dwelling has geraniums cascading brightly from each windowsill, and looks directly onto Sciliar mountain out of the back. The guestrooms are simply furnished with light pinewood beds and side tables, and only one has its own bathroom. The breakfast room overlooks the town and a small swimming pool, which is a welcome feature indeed on hot summer afternoons or after a day of hiking. *Directions:* Exit at Bolzano Nord from Verona-Brennero autostrada. Follow signs for Siusi and Fie (also called Vols) and, at main intersection, turn right to Merlhof.

MERLHOF
Hosts: Maria Kompatscher family
Via Sciliar 14
Fie allo Sciliar (Vols) (BZ) 39050, Italy
tel: (0471) 725092
7 rooms, 1 with private bathroom
Lire 25,000 per person B&B
Breakfast only
Open all year
No English spoken (German)
Region: Alto Adige

The Hotel Aprile, owned by the Cantini Zucconi family for the past 35 years, is located in a 15th-century Medici palace behind the Piazza Santa Maria Novella, near the train station and many fine restaurants and shops. The historical building was restored under the strict ordinance of Florence's Commission of Fine Arts. The small and charming hotel is full of delightful surprises: from 16th-century paintings and a bust of the Duke of Tuscany to the frescoed breakfast room and quiet courtyard garden. The old-fashioned reception and sitting areas are invitingly furnished with Florentine renaissance antiques, comfy overstuffed red armchairs and oriental carpets worn with time. The wallpapered bedrooms include telephone and minibar, and feature parquet floors and high vaulted ceilings, but vary widely in their size and decor; some are too basic and modern. There are twenty-four doubles with private bathrooms, and another five which share two bathrooms just outside the rooms. Request one of the quieter rooms at the back of the hotel, overlooking the garden. *Directions:* Use a detailed city map to locate the hotel, three blocks north of the Duomo. There is a parking garage.

HOTEL APRILE
Hosts: Valeria Cantini Zucconi family
Via della Scala 6
Florence 50123, Italy
tel: (055) 216237; fax: (055) 280947
29 rooms, 24 with private bathrooms
Lire 170,000 double B&B
Breakfast only
Credit cards: all major
Open all year
English spoken well
Region: Tuscany

The relaxed and friendly Ariele Hotel has been in the Bertelloni family for the past 40 years. Located in a quiet residential section across from the Opera House, it is within a short walking distance to the center of town. The entrance and reception area is made up of several old-fashioned style sitting rooms, giving an immediate sense of the private home it used to be (which dates back to 14th Century). These spaces include a breakfast room and wall-papered sitting room with antique reproductions, gold velvet armchairs, fireplace, and oriental carpets on tiled floors. A pleasant side garden with white iron-wrought tables and chairs offers a shady spot for breakfast. There is also space here for parking and hidden off in a corner is an unusual independent double room. The spacious, high-ceilinged rooms are individually decorated using a mix of old and new furnishings and have either wood parquet or marble floors. Unfortunately the florescent lighting does not help brighten up the sometimes drab color scheme. Guests can depend on the kind assistance of the staff for restaurant and itinerary suggestions. *Directions:* Between Piazza Vittorio Veneto and the Arno river. Use a detailed city map to locate the hotel.

HOTEL ARIELE
Hosts: Bertelloni family
Via Magenta 11
Florence 50123, Italy
tel: (055) 211509; fax: (055) 26852
40 rooms with private bathrooms
Lire 165,000 double B&B
Breakfast only
Credit cards: VS
Open all year
English spoken well
Region: Tuscany

If you are facing the Florence train station, a block to the right is the Via Fiume. At the end of this tranquil street is the Hotel Desiree, located on the upper floors of a building (as is typical of city pensione) and owned and operated by gracious Graziella Pili. Eighteen double rooms are contained within, off a long, gleaming marble hallway wide enough to include a desk and two overstuffed armchairs. Each room has a new bathroom, high ceiling, patterned, polished tile floor, TV and telephone. The guestrooms are simply decorated with painted furniture and the occasional antique. From the small entrance area, stained glass doors lead to the sweet breakfast room with its pink linen tablecloths topped with fresh bouquets, and out onto its flower-laden balcony overlooking the famous terra-cotta rooftops of Florence—among them that belonging to the glorious Duomo. Signora Pili takes visible pride in her newly renovated hotel and keeps it in immaculate condition. The two-star Hotel Desiree maintains high standards and an economical rate, a combination not easy to find. *Directions:* Use a detailed city map to locate. Parking facilities are available.

HOTEL DESIREE
Hosts: Graziella Pili & Ferdinando Cellini
Via Fiume 20
Florence 50123, Italy
tel & fax: (055) 2382382
18 rooms with private bathrooms
Lire 120,000 double B&B
Breakfast only
Credit cards: VS,MC
Open all year
Some English spoken
Region: Tuscany

The Hotel Hermitage is the kind of accommodation travelers dream about finding in this magical city. It is a small, well-manicured hotel with efficient service and breathtaking views over the city's most famous monuments. The location could not be more central on a small street between the Uffizzi gallery and the Arno River. Housed in a 13th-century palazzo, the 5th floor reception area is a polished and cozy room with selected antique pieces, looking out to the Ponte Vecchio bridge. Across the hall is the veranda-like breakfast room dotted with crisp yellow tablecloths and topped with fresh flowers where privileged guests view the tower of Palazzo Signoria. Color-coordinated rooms, recently renovated, have scattered antiques, framed etchings of the city and more views. However, the highlight of a stay at the Hermitage is spending time dreaming on the rooftop terrace. It not only includes the previously mentioned marvels of Florence, but the dome of the Duomo and Giotto's tower as well. Guests are served breakfast under the ivy-covered pergola and among the many flower-laden vases lining its borders—simply intoxicating. Reserve well in advance. *Directions:* Consult a detailed city map.

HOTEL HERMITAGE
Director: Vincenzo Scarcelli
Piazza del Pesce
Florence 50122, Italy
tel: (055) 287216; fax: (055) 212208
29 rooms with private bathrooms
Lire 160,000-210,000 double B&B
Breakfast only
Credit cards: VS, MC
Open all year
English spoken well
Region: Tuscany

It is not hard to find accommodations in a 15th-century palace in downtown Florence; the historical center of the city has little else. The Residenza is no exception, but it features the added attraction of being situated on Florence's most elegant street, the *Tornabuoni*. For the last fifteen years the gracious Giacalone family has occupied the palazzo's top three floors and operated them as a pensione (now a hotel). An antique elevator takes you up to the reception area, which opens onto a pretty dining room with pink tablecloths and shelves lined with a collection of bottles, vases and ceramics. Twenty-four comfortably worn, very simply furnished rooms are divided between the next two floors (the upper floor being the most desirable), capped with a rooftop terrace burgeoning with flowerpots and surrounded by city views. Room decor differs quite a bit as they are in the gradual process of being upgraded with good antique reproductions. A comfortable sitting room with high, beamed ceilings and a television for guests is located on the upper floor. La Residenza is one of the few small hotels offering dinner on the premises, and the proprietors are justifiably proud of their reputation for serving authentic Florentine cuisine. *Directions:* Use a detailed city map to locate the hotel in the heart of Florence.

LA RESIDENZA
Hosts: Gianna & Paolo (son) Giacalone
Via Tornabuoni 8
Florence 50123, Italy
tel & fax: (055) 284197
24 rooms with private bathrooms
Lire 185,000 double B&B
Breakfast and dinner served
Credit cards: all major
Open all year
English spoken well
Region: Tuscany

The newly refurbished Hotel Silla is located on the left bank of the Arno River opposite Santa Croce, the famous 13th-century square and church where Michelangelo and Galileo are buried. This position offers views from some of the rooms of several of Florence's most notable architectural attractions—the Duomo, the Ponte Vecchio and the tower of Palazzo Vecchio. Housed on the second and third floors of a lovely 15th-century palazzo with courtyard entrance, thirty very new and spotless double rooms with private baths are pleasantly decorated with simple dark wood furniture and matching bedspreads and curtains. The fancy cream-colored reception area is appointed in 17th-century Venetian style, with period furniture, chandelier and large paintings. Breakfast is served on the splendid and spacious second floor outdoor terrace or in the dining room overlooking the Arno. The Silla is a friendly, convenient and quiet hotel, near the Pitti Palace, leather artisan shops and many restaurants. It offers tourists a good value in pricey Florence. Air-conditioned rooms and garage service available. *Directions:* Refer to a detailed city map to locate the hotel.

HOTEL SILLA
Host: Gabriele Belotti
Via dei Renai 5
Florence 50125, Italy
tel: (055) 2342888; fax: (055) 2341437
32 rooms, 30 with private bathrooms
Lire 170,000 double B&B
Breakfast only
Credit cards: all major
Open all year
English spoken well
Region: Tuscany

The Hotel Splendor is exactly as its name implies—splendid. Traffic and street noise is a common problem in the bustling urban center of Florence, but the Splendor, off on a quiet side street, manages to miss most of it. Yet guests won't miss being able to walk almost everywhere, since the hotel is only three blocks from the Duomo and near the Accademia museum where the *David* is found. The prim, centuries-old palazzo, of the pale-yellow hue characteristic of Florence, has geranium-filled boxes at every window. The ambiance is reminiscent of a time-worn elegant private home (which the palazzo was until 1957), with its frescoed foyer and sitting rooms graced with portraits, chandeliers, overstuffed armchairs and oriental carpets. In the summer months, the perfume of the family's own garden roses—found throughout the hotel—fills the air. On the second and third floors are the thirty-one spacious guestrooms, (some can sleep a family of four), most were recently redecorated with lovely matching armoires and beds in typical Florentine painted pastel style. Perhaps the architectural highlight is the gracious breakfast room, with high ceilings, parquet floors and frescoed panels all around. French doors lead from this area to an outdoor terrace with white iron chairs and tables where guests may take in a lovely view of San Marco church while enjoying a superb buffet breakfast. Daughter Mariangela offers special attention to guest's needs. Garage service also available. *Directions:* Rely on a detailed city map to locate the hotel.

HOTEL SPLENDOR
Hosts: Vincenzo Masoero family
Via San Gallo 30
Florence 50129, Italy
tel: (055) 483427; fax: (055) 461276
31 rooms, 25 with private bathrooms
Lire 160,000 double B&B, 120,000 without bath
Breakfast only
Credit cards: VS,MC
Open all year
English spoken well
Region: Tuscany

On the hillside above Florence, famous for its fantastic city views, is one of the many beautiful properties related to the noble Corsini family. This particular estate is comprised of an enormous castle, smaller villas, a convent, individual houses for the servants, and hundreds of acres of olive groves and hilly countryside (including Monte Cerceri where Da Vinci conducted his experiments with flight). The 15th-century castle, where scenes from the film, *Room with a View,* were filmed, is rented out for weddings and special occasions. Its enclosed front lawn provides a superb view over the unique rooftops of Florence. The Corsini's are in the process of restoring the convent and smaller houses to accommodate guests, and currently offer two apartments for weekly stays. Simple, more basic rooms are available, but the superior one has a large living/dining area with upstairs loft/bedroom and a kitchenette tastefully decorated with antiques and personal belongings of the family. An excellent restaurant on the property serves typical Florentine dishes, while a small grocery store on site sells enough of the farm's own fresh produce (cheese, wine, olive oil) to prepare a simple self-catered meal. *Directions:* From Florence follow signs for Fiesole. Cross through downtown and start descent back to Florence on villa-lined road. The Maiano is on the first curve on the left.

FATTORIA DI MAIANO
Host: Francesco Mari Fulcis
Via Benedetto da Maiano 11
Fiesole (FI) 50016, Italy
tel: (055) 599600; fax: (055) 599640
2 apartments
Lire 900,000-1,200,000 weekly
Trattoria on premises
Credit cards: VS
Open all year
English spoken well
Region: Tuscany

For the fortunate travelers with time to explore the rich treasures of Florence and the spectacular surrounding countryside as well, innumerable surprises await them. On the extreme outskirts of the city, the Fattoressa offers the ideal location for this type of "dual" exploration. One of the many marvelous attractions of Florence is how the countryside comes right up to the doors of the city. Just behind the magnificent Certosa monastery is situated the 15th-century stone farmhouse of the delightfully congenial Fusi-Borgioli family. With loving care, they have transformed the farmer's quarters into guest accommodations: four sweetly simple bedrooms, each with its own spotless bathroom. Running a bed and breakfast seems to come naturally to Angelina and Amelio, who treat their guests like family and as a result, enjoy receiving some of them year after year. Visitors take meals *en famille* at long tables in the cozy, rustic dining room with large stone fireplace. Here Angelina proudly serves authentic Florentine specialties using ingredients from her own fruit orchard and vegetable garden. *Directions:* Entering Florence from Certosa exit off Siena superstrada, turn left one street after the Certosa Convent. After the bridge, turn right behind the building (Via Volterrana—slightly hidden). The house is just on left.

PODERE LA FATTORESSA
Hosts: Angelina Fusi & Amelio Borgioli
Via Volterrana 58
Galluzzo (FI) 50124, Italy
tel: (055) 2048418
4 rooms with private bathrooms
Lire 120,000 double B&B
Breakfast and dinner served
Open all year
No English spoken
Region: Tuscany

A very pleasant alternative to hotels in Florence is a stay at the Milione wine estate in the hills overlooking the city. Signor Brandimarte, besides running a successful silver-making business, and being a sculptor, oversees this expansive farm property with its large olive oil and wine production as well. Many rooms and apartments are divided among the main villa and another complex of stone farmhouses a short distance down the road. They are well decorated with lovely country antiques, terra-cotta brick floors, beamed ceilings and dried flower bouquets. Each room varies in size and decor, many are equipped with kitchenette and eating area. Most have wonderful views over the soft hills lined with vineyards. The swimming pool is surrounded by terra-cotta vases filled with geraniums and other seasonal plants and bordered by a wood-paneled house with changing rooms for the convenience of guests. Fresh bread and homemade jam are provided for breakfast daily in all rooms. Dinner may be served upon request, which is taken together around one long table. The combination of being immersed in the peaceful countryside while having Florence spread out before you below, makes Il Milione an idyllic B&B choice. *Directions:* Exit from autostrada at Certosa. Follow for center city and turn left at Galluzzo. Follow the road for 2 km and turn a sharp right at sign for Rossi Ristorante.

IL MILIONE
Hosts: Brandimarte Family
Via di Giogoli 14
Florence 50124, Italy
tel: (055) 2048713
4 rooms with private bathrooms
5 apartments
Lire 110,000 double B&B
3-day minimum stay
All meals served
Open all year
English spoken well
Region: Tuscany

The Castello di Tornano is a very special place to stay for those wishing to explore in depth the rich culture of this extraordinary region. The strategically situated hilltop tower, dating back almost 1,000 years, has a 360-degree vista of the surrounding valley and has been of great historical significance in the seemingly endless territorial battles between the Siena and Florence. Given how ancient the property is, it is incredible to discover that the current owners, the Selvolini family from Florence, are only the third proprietors. Patrizia and Barbara, the family's lovely daughters, opened the wine estate to guests five years ago. Weekly stays begin with a cocktail party around the exquisite pool cut into the rock and spanned by a bridge. Eight simply appointed suites, each with living area, kitchen, one or two bedrooms and garden, are situated in a stone farmhouse in front of the tower. The *pièce de résistance*, however, is the three-floor apartment within the monumental tower, impeccably furnished in grand style and featuring three bedrooms, two living rooms with fireplace, dining room, kitchen and tower-top terrace with a view not easily forgotten. Meals can be taken at the restaurant on the property. *Directions:* From Siena follow signs for Gaiole (25 km). Continue past town for 5 km. Just past Lecchi turnoff (on left), turn right for Tornano-Guarnelotto Ristorante.

CASTELLO DI TORNANO
Hosts: Patrizia & Barbara Selvolini
Localita: Lecchi
Gaiole in Chianti (SI) 53013, Italy
tel: (0577) 746067; fax: (055) 6580818
9 apartments
Lire 650,000 to 2,500,000 (tower) weekly
Trattoria on premises
Credit cards: AX, DC
Open Easter-October and Christmas
English spoken very well
Region: Tuscany

Traveling south along the heel of Italy, you will encounter a wealth of natural beauty, but because far off the beaten trail, few really charming places to stay. The Masseria lo Prieno is run by the delightful Castriota family, who has owned the farm for three generations. The Castriota's crops are representative of the staples of the Apulia region, and include olives, almonds, fruits and grains. Spartan accommodations are offered in bungalows scattered among the pine woods and palms on the family property. Each guest house includes two bedrooms, kitchen, bathroom and an eating area containing basic necessities. What were formerly animal stalls have been converted into a large dining space rustically decorated with antique farm tools and brass pots. Along with warm hospitality, the family makes the kitchen's offerings a top priority. For an exquisite and authentic traditional meal, the restaurant here is incomparable. Both Maria Grazia, the energetic daughter who runs the show, and her charming mother take pride in demonstrating how local specialties are prepared: from fresh pastas to breads and desserts. Dinner here is truly something special. *Directions:* From Taranto take N174 to Galatone, then follow signs for Secli. Turn right on Via Gramsci, then left on Via San Luca. Follow signs for Lo Prieno. 80 km from Brindisi.

MASSERIA LO PRIENO
Hosts: Francesco Castriota family
Localita: Contrada Orelle
Galatone (LE) 73044, Italy
tel: (0833) 861391 / 865443
fax: (0833) 282859
9 bungalows
Lire 50,000 per person half board
Breakfast and dinner served
Open April-September
Credit cards: VS
Some English spoken
Region: Apulia

Cozy accommodations are hard to come by in the beautiful lake area of Garda, so it was a particular pleasure to discover the utterly delightful Ca'Vescova bed and breakfast, lovingly owned and operated by the Russo family. Besides being responsible for the culinary work, multi-talented Monica is an excellent gardener and horsewoman. She breeds and trains horses, and conducts outings with guests (western saddle). Darling son, Davide, eagerly shows guests around while Monica's brother, Zeno, welcomes guests and tends to the farm animals and vegetable garden which supply the kitchen. The salmon-colored farmhouse sits peacefully on a hillside surrounded by vineyards and a panorama of the lake and town of Garda below. Guests have a separate entrance to the seven small rooms on the second and third floors. All bedrooms have modern bathrooms, and are simply decorated with country antiques and old-world prints. Sister Barbara serves breakfast, either on the flowered terrace or in the polished country-style dining room, accented by colorful ceramic cups and pitchers lining the shelves and fireplace mantle. Just 45 km north of Verona, this is an excellent base for touring the Veneto region. *Directions:* From Verona take either the scenic lakeside route to Garda or the direct A22 autostrada toward Brennero and exit at Affi-Garda. Follow signs for Costermano, pass through town, then turn right on Via Per Marciaga. Under 2 hrs to both Milan airports.

CA'VESCOVA
Hosts: Monica, Barbara & Zeno Russo
Via Per Marciago 18
Garda (VR) 37016, Italy
tel: (045) 7255057; fax: (045) 7256785
7 rooms with private bathrooms
Lire 120,000 double B&B
* 75,000 per person half board*
Breakfast lunch and dinner served
Credit cards: all major
Open Easter-October
English spoken well
Region: Veneto

The Casa Nova B&B, in relation to our other more remote selections in the area, has the advantage of being on the edge of Greve, the center of the Chianti region. Although the newer section of town is being built practically outside the front door, the large hilly property covered with vineyards seems deep in the countryside. Any new construction is absolutely invisible from the house. Sandra Taccetti and her husband decided to leave their stone farmhouse with six bedrooms for their guests, while they converted the barn into their own living quarters. There is a simple and casual feel to the place and guests can be right at home in the downstairs living room with its floral-print sofas, breakfast room, or out on the back porch overlooking the garden and lush green landscape. The clean and uncluttered bedrooms, all with bathrooms except one, are appropriately decorated with country antiques. The beamed ceilings and brick floors naturally make up the rest of the decor. The two adjoining rooms with sharing bathroom are ideal for a family of four, while two other doubles each have their own terrace. From Casa Nova you are equidistant to Florence and Siena. *Directions:* From Florence coming into town, turn left at first stoplight, Via Gramsci and follow curve up to the left. The road ends at the house. *Note:* Via Uzzano has nothing to do with signs for Castello di Uzzano.

CASA NOVA
Hostess: Sandra Taccetti
Via di Uzzano 30
Greve in Chianti (FI) 50022, Italy
tel: (055) 853459
6 rooms, 5 with private bathrooms
Lire 100,000 double B&B
Breakfast only
Open all year
Very little English spoken
Region: Tuscany

Set deep in the heart of the Chianti region, this rambling white villa with terra-cotta roof dominates the surrounding valley of olive trees and grape vines. Arminio Gericke, a Tuscan of German origin, made his home here over 25 years ago, and is as dedicated to the art of producing fine wines and olive oil as he is to providing hospitality to his guests. Arminio has managed to retain the villa's 18th-century character, splendidly visible in the high-ceiling, frescoed salon with piano and fireplace. In one wing are the seven bedrooms, three with private bath, each decorated differently and simply with wrought-iron beds and original antiques. Also within the villa are five spacious apartments accommodating two to eight people and available by the week. Breakfast is taken downstairs in the rustic dining room off the large kitchen with cook-in fireplace. Just before the villa is a group of stone houses containing *La Cantinetta* restaurant offering excellent farm-fresh specialties. An extra plus is the picturesque swimming pool surrounded by olive trees. Tennis, horseback riding and golf are available nearby. *Directions:* Take Tavernelle exit off the Siena-Firenze superstrada. Follow signs for Passignano and, just after the abbey, turn right on a gravel road and follow signs to Rignana (12 km).

FATTORIA DI RIGNANA
Host: Dottor Arminio Gericke
Localita: Rignana
Greve in Chianti (FI) 50022, Italy
tel: (055) 852065; fax: (O55) 598729
7 rooms, 3 with private bathrooms
5 apartments
Lire 110,000 double B&B
Trattoria on premises
Credit cards: AX
Open Easter-October
Some English spoken
Region: Tuscany

What happens when four young and ambitious Italian men from various regions of the country pool their earnings and restaurant experience to open a country inn? You can see for yourself by visiting the recently opened Borgo Antico. In the remote, rugged back hills of Chianti, on the highest peak of Monte San Michele, is a cluster of stone houses dating from 1300 that the energetic foursome is gradually and meticulously restoring according to antique drawings. Naturally they began with the restaurant, which emphasizes fine cuisine prepared from the freshest ingredients. Claudio and Eralio busily create in the kitchen, while Massimo and Walter host the two intimate dining rooms accented with crisp pink tablecloths. During the warmer months, regulars know to request the outdoor terrace with grape arbor overlooking the brilliant green landscape. Four guest rooms have been fashioned in the tower (one per floor, with bathrooms just outside each), with future plans for others soon. The rooms are simply but tastefully appointed with antique armoires and colorful floral bedspreads. *Directions:* Take Incisa exit off the Florence-Siena highway. Follow signs for Greve, after 14 km, (Greve is 10 km beyond) turn left for Lucolena/Monte San Michele and follow road up mountain 7 km.

LOCANDA BORGO ANTICO
Hosts: Claudio, Walter, Massimo, Eralio
Localita: Lucolena
Greve in Chianti (FI) 50022, Italy
tel: (055) 851024
4 rooms with private bathrooms
Lire 70,000 double B&B
All meals served (closed Tuesdays)
Credit cards: VS,MC
Open Easter-October
English spoken well
Region: Tuscany

The very simple but economical Oasi Verde or "green oasis" is just that; a convenient roadside B&B for those leaving Umbria towards the Marches region or vice versa. Carla and Andrea Rossi, the young couple who started the B&B and restaurant activity four years ago, inherited the sprawling 200-year-old stone farmhouse and surrounding land. Its ideal location midway between Perugia and Gubbio (a not-to-be-missed medieval stone village), plus reputation for good local cuisine, made it a sure bet from the start. The eight rooms each with own bathroom will eventually be decorated like model room no. 3, with its original beamed ceiling and antique bed and armoire. For the present, the others are rather void of personality, spartan but clean, having white tiled floors, pine paneled walls and modern beds. Another wing of the complex houses 3 apartments for longer stays, perfect for a family of four. The windows at the back of the house open out to the green hills with alternating square patches of woods and sunflower fields. The facilities have been recently enhanced by the addition of a swimming pool. *Directions:* From Perugia on rte 298 after 25 km, B&B on left side, at Mengara, 10 km outside Gubbio.

OASI VERDE
Hosts: Andrea & Carla Rossi
Localita: Mengara 1
Gubbio (PG) 06024, Italy
tel: (075) 920156
8 rooms with private bathrooms, 3 apartments
Lire 85,000 double B&B
3 day minimum stay (high season)
All meals served
Open all year
Very little English spoken
Region: Umbria

Just 18 km from Florence, tucked away on a hilltop in Chianti, is the marvelous convent of San Niccolo d'Olmeto consisting of a medieval tower, Romanesque church and Renaissance cloister. The Cavagnari family, with their architecture and hotelier background, (they own and run the J and J Hotel in Florence), took on the very ambitious task of restoring the dilapidated buildings to their original beauty. The peaceful and enchanting setting with its surrounding woods, vineyards and olive groves, makes this accommodation a perfect spot for dreamers. Five rooms in the main villa, each with ensuite bathroom, are showcases for the family's antique and art collection which blend in effectively with more modern light fixtures and furniture. Clever architectural tricks are incorporated into the historic stone structure to create divisions between rooms, arched doorways and a bridge in the tower. Gorgeous views of the countryside are captured from every little window. In another part of the complex are four suites for 2-3 persons decorated with more fine antique pieces. These are rented out by the week and include their own equipped kitchenette. An added plus is the swimming pool beside the rose garden. (Reservations are made through the hotel). *Directions:* Exit at Incisa from A1 autostrada and head north on rte 69. Pass Burchio and watch for small yellow sign on left side.

SAN NICCOLO D'OLMETO
Hosts: Cavagnari Family
Localita: Le Valli
Incisa Val d'Arno (FI) 50066, Italy
tel: (055) 240951; fax: (055) 240282
5 rooms with private bathrooms
5 suites for weekly rental
Lire 140,000 double B&B
  600,000-900,000 weekly for suites
Breakfast and dinner upon request
Open April-October
English spoken very well
Region: Tuscany

Just south of the fascinating Etruscan/medieval villages of Montemerano, Sovana and Saturnia (well-known for the 2,000-year-old hot springs), is this isolated B&B situated within a national park. A cluster of stone buildings, neglected for decades, was once a community serving the castle down the road. This is where two extraordinarily determined Dutch women decided to settle, and the results of their renovating efforts are truly miraculous. Six guestrooms have been tastefully fashioned in one part of the sectioned farmhouse, each with its own distinct personality and color scheme. Special marbling techniques have been applied to the walls in warm earth tones, lending an intimate feeling to the rooms. Antique furniture mixes well with wicker pieces, enhanced by the rich terra-cotta floors and beamed ceilings. A minor dilemma of how to make a windowless passageway appealing was resolved by importing an Austrian surrealistic painter to fresco the walls, floor, and ceiling. The trompe d'oeil effect is like walking onto a terrace on a romantic starry night. Other amenities include a cozy kitchen and a library for guests. In the vicinity are horse stables and a golf course. *Directions:* From Rome (1-1/2 hours away), take the Aurelia road to Vulci, follow signs for Manciano. Campigliola is on the left, 9 km before town.

CAMPIGLIOLA COUNTRY CLUB
Hosts: Frida Van der Horst & P.J. Van den Bergh
Localita: Campigliola, Manciano (GR) 58014, Italy
tel & fax: (0564) 629194
6 rooms with private bathrooms
Lire 114,000 double B&B; 150,000 triple B&B
2-day minimum stay
Breakfast only
Credit cards: VS
Open March-January
English spoken well
Region: Tuscany

When the parents of Florentine sisters Francesca and Beatrice Baccetti proposed to let them take over the family's country home and vineyards, and convert the property into a B&B, they eagerly accepted the challenge. Restoration work began immediately on the two adjacent stone buildings dating back to 1400. All original architectural features were preserved, leaving the five guestrooms and ten apartments (for 2 to 4 people) with clay-tiled floors, wood-beamed ceilings, mansard roofs, and generous views over the tranquil Tuscan countryside. The very comfortable and tidy rooms are furnished with good reproductions and feel almost hotel-like, with telephone, television and modern bathrooms in each. A swimming pool, tennis courts, billiards room, and nearby horse stables are at the guests' disposal, although finding enough to do is hardly a problem with Florence only 18 km away and practically all of Tuscany at one's fingertips. Lingering over breakfast, served at wood tables in the stone-walled dining room (or out on the terrace), allows the opportunity to chat with either Francesca or Beatrice, both very outgoing and knowledgeable on their native area. Readers give Salvadonica a high rating. *Directions:* From Florence take the superstrada toward Siena, exiting at San Casciano Nord. Follow signs for town, taking a left at the sign for Mercatale. Salvadonica is on this road and well-marked.

SALVADONICA
Hosts: Francesca & Beatrice Baccetti
Via Grevigiana 82
Mercatale Val di Pesa (FI) 50024, Italy
tel: (055) 8218039; fax: (055) 8218043
5 rooms with private bathrooms, 10 apartments
Lire 120,000 double B&B
Breakfast only
Credit cards: all major
Open March-October
English spoken very well
Region: Tuscany

While many agriturismo farms are run by transplanted urbanites, many are still owned and operated by farmers whose families have worked the land for generations. Such is the case with Onofrio Contento and his family, proprietors of Masseria Curatori, not far from the city of Monopoli and the sea. The three studious, red-headed sons (evidence of Apulia's Norman invasion) assist their father with chores on the farm, where for five generations, the family has produced olives, almonds and cattle. Inside the main coral-color house are modest and immaculate quarters for guests, consisting presently of two, two-bedroom apartments with kitchens, one double with bath, and two doubles sharing a bath. Old and new family furniture have been combined to decorate the rooms. The view is pleasingly pastoral, overlooking olive tree studded hills. Several new rooms have just been completed in a nearby building overlooking a lovely stone-walled garden and fruit orchard. Breakfast and extra meals are taken together with the family in their dining room. Horseback riding is also arranged for guests. Recommended for visitors with some command of the Italian language. This inn is very near the Adriatic Sea. *Directions:* 40 km from Brindisi. Take coastal route N16, exiting at Monopoli-San Francesco da Paola. Take road back across highway and make first left. Follow Via Conchia for 2 km to the pink house.

MASSERIA CURATORI
Hosts: Onofrio Contento family
Contrada Cristo delle Zolle 227
Monopoli (BA) 70043, Italy
tel: (080) 777472
4 rooms with private bathrooms, 4 apartments
Lire 60,000 double B&B
* 50,000 per person half board*
Breakfast lunch and dinner served
2-day minimum stay
Open all year
Very little English spoken
Region: Apulia

More than a cursory visit to the culturally rich region of Veneto, with its Palladio villas and enchanting towns such as Verona, Vicenza and Padua, will handsomely reward the effort. Just south of Padua, outside the medieval town of Monselice with its imposing castle, is the family-run B&B of Silvia Sagradin and family. Ten years ago they restored the late-19th-century farmhouse, converting the stables into a large airy restaurant equipped with long family-style wooden tables and copper pots hanging from the ceiling. Judging from the number of patrons, it is apparent that the eatery has become a favorite Sunday outing for both rural and urban folk, largely due to the superior country cuisine served there. The entire family is involved in the effort, either as hosts, working in the fruit orchards, or on site in the busy kitchen, where it seems fresh pasta is being prepared at all hours. For guests wishing to stay overnight, two rooms have recently been incorporated into the house. Ideal for a family of four, this separate section of the house includes the two bedrooms (decorated with inherited country furniture, lace curtains and beamed ceilings) newly built bathroom and a small private dining area. Overwhelmed by the number of visitors coming to her through our guide, gregarious (but slightly frustrated) Silvia is taking a crash course in English! *Directions:* Take the A13 autostrada south toward Ferrara, exiting at Monselice, then follow the yellow signs to Molini, 20 km from Padua.

FATTORIA SAVELLON MOLINI
Hosts: Silvia Sagradin & family
Via Savellon Molini
Monselice (PD) 35042, Italy
tel: (0429) 73135 / 782212
2 rooms sharing a bathroom
Lire 70,000 double B&B
 45,000 per person half board
All meals served
Open Easter-September
Very little English spoken
Region: Veneto

Traveling southwest toward Florence through the foothills of the Appenines, the scenery transforms itself dramatically from the flatlands of the *padana* into soft green hills textured with alternating fields of wheat and grape vines. From Bologna, the Tenuta Bonzara farm and vineyard is a half hour drive up a road that winds through scented pine forest, arriving at a group of houses owned by several farming families. The wine estate is owned by Dottore Lambertini of Bologna, and is run by warm-hearted Mario and his family, whose main responsibility is overseeing the wine production. Guest accommodation on the estate consists of two small houses containing two apartments, each with one or two bedrooms, bathroom, kitchenette and sitting room. Preferred are the one-bedroom apartments in the older house with small corner fireplaces, red-brick floors and beamed ceilings, rustically furnished with simple pinewood pieces. A trattoria on the premises serves meals, and an interesting museum has been set up in the old barn displaying antique farm tools, carts, and agricultural machines. Horseback riding is available, and participation in the grape harvesting is encouraged. *Directions:* Take Bologna/Casalecchio exit from the A1 autostrada, and continue to Gesso, Rivabella, San Chierlo and Monte San Pietro, where you go left up the hill.

TENUTA BONZARA
Host: Dottor Francesco Lambertini
Via San Chierlo 37
Monte San Pietro (BO) 40050, Italy
tel: (051) 6768324; fax: (051) 225772
4 apartments
Lire 500,000 weekly
3-day minimum stay in low season
Trattoria on premises (dinner only)
Open May-October
Some English spoken
Region: Emilia-Romagna

The scenic approach to the Fattoria di Vibio passes through lush green hills, by picturesque farms, and is highlighted by a romantic view of the quaint town of Todi, 20 km away, setting the mood for an enjoyable stay. This is a top-drawer bed and breakfast consisting of several recently restored stone houses, and manning the operation are two handsome brothers from Rome. The houses sit side by side and share between them ten double rooms with private baths. Common areas for guests include a cozy, country-style living room with fireplace, game room and country kitchen. The accommodations are enhanced by preserved architectural features such as terra-cotta floors and exposed-beam ceilings. Typical Umbrian handicrafts such as wrought-iron beds, renovated antiques, and *Deruta* ceramics are evident. On the assumption that guests may find it difficult to leave this haven, the hosts offer half-board, along with a beautiful swimming pool, tennis, hiking and horseback riding and biking. Signora Gabriella, with a passion for cooking, gets all the richly deserved credit for the marvelous meals served either poolside or on the panoramic terrace. *Directions:* From either Todi or Orvieto follow route S448 until turnoff for Vibio just outside Todi. Follow well-marked dirt road for 10 km.

FATTORIA DI VIBIO
Hosts: Giuseppe Saladini & Gabriella Moscati
Localita: Buchella-Doglio
San Venanzo (TR) 05010, Italy
tel: (075) 8749607; fax: (075) 8780014
10 rooms with private bathrooms
Lire 110,000 double B&B
* 110,000 per person half board*
2-day minimum stay
Breakfast and dinner served
Credit cards: VS, AX
Open Easter-November
Very little English spoken
Region: Umbria

For those who wish for accommodations with all the trimmings, yet still want to feel like a pampered guest in a private home, Villa Pambuffetti is an ideal choice. Situated in Umbria, the "green heart" of Italy, in the well-preserved hilltop town of Montefalco with its 13th-century Francescano frescoes, this splendid villa opened its doors to guests one year ago. The decision to transform the family's country house into a 15-room inn was made naturally when gracious Signora Pambuffetti's daughter, Alessandra, and husband Mauro, returned from the States with a "baggage full" of experience in the hotel/restaurant business. Alessandra demonstrates her culinary skills preparing Umbrian specialties for guests with her own flair. Her delicious cakes, tarts, and homemade jams are part of the full breakfast served in the elegant cream and dusty rose colored dining room. Here guests are treated to the same spectacular panoramic view taking in Assisi, Perugia, Spoleto, Spello, as described by Herman Hesse in 1907. The actual villa is also mentioned, with its manicured gardens (now with swimming pool), and centuries-old cypress trees. Every small detail is tended to in the individually-decorated rooms with their marble travertine bathrooms. The room in the tower, named the *torre dell'amore* with its 360-degree vistas is a favorite among honeymooners. *Directions:* From the Perugia-Spoleto superstrada, turn for Montefalco at Borgo Trevi and follow signs once in town.

VILLA PAMBUFFETTI
Hosts: Pambuffetti family
Via della Vittoria 20
Montefalco (PG) 06036, Italy
tel: (0742) 79417; fax: (0742) 79245
15 rooms with private bathrooms
Lire 200,000-230,000 double B&B
All meals served
Credit cards: all major
Open all year
English spoken very well
Region: Umbria

Surprisingly, one of the least visited regions in Italy is the Marches, an area rich in culture, nature and history, bordered by the Adriatic on one side and Emilia-Romangna, Umbria and Abruzzo on the other. Just 15 km from the coast in the heart of this gentle, hilly countryside, is the Campana farm, run by 10 families of professionals and artists (architect, painter, designer, poet, doctor) who came here from Milan 10 years ago in search of an alternative lifestyle. The farm, made up of four pale-peach stone houses dating from 1700, has been restored with great care and taste, making space for private quarters, a refined restaurant, wine cellar, studio, music room and for guests, two double rooms and an apartment with two bedrooms. The latter has lovely terraces looking across vineyard-covered hills to the distant sea, and are decorated with a combination of old and new furnishings. Drawing on the considerable pool of available talent, an unusual variety of activities is offered—from courses in painting, theater, sculpture and photography to workshops in crafting leather, silk and wool. A swimming pool and tennis courts were recently added. *Directions:* From Ancona go south on the A14 autostrada, exit at Pedaso and continue south to Carassai, then turn right. After 5 km, turn right for Montefiore, then left at the small sign for La Campana.

LA CAMPANA
Hosts: Coop Agricola
Via Menocchia 39
Montefiore d'Aso (AP) 63010, Italy
tel: (0734) 938229; fax: (0734) 938484
2 rooms and 1 apartment with private bathrooms
Lire 95,000 double B&B
  65,000 per person half board
Breakfast and dinner served
Open all year
English spoken well
Region: Marches

La Loggia, built in 1427, was one of the Medici estates during the centuries they ruled over Florence and surrounding territories. Owner Giulio Baruffaldi, formerly an architect, and art dealer, weary of urban life in Milan, transplanted himself and his wife here years ago. He has succeeded in reviving the estate's splendor while respecting its past. They've enhanced its architectural beauty while giving utmost attention to comforts and warmth. Their commitment to informal yet refined hospitality is evident in the care given to the decor of the apartment-suites, each containing one to three bedrooms, living room, kitchen, fireplace and many lovely antiques and original paintings from the Baruffaldi's own art collection. In fact, many important bronze and ceramic sculptures by international artists are displayed throughout the gardens of the villa. Apart from just basking in the pure romance and tranquillity of this place, there is a swimming pool, horseback riding, and nearby tennis and golf facilities. Other activities include the occasional cooking or wine-tasting lesson, and impromptu dinners in the cellar. The hosts and their absolutely charming guest assistant, Ivana, seem to exist merely to pamper their guests' every whim. This is the stuff dreams are made of. *Directions:* From the Florence-Siena autostrada exit after San Casciano at Bargino. Turn right at end of ramp, then left for Montefiridolfi (3.5 km). La Loggia is just outside town.

FATTORIA LA LOGGIA
Hosts: Giulio Baruffaldi & Cuca Roaldi
Via Collina, Montefiridolfi in Chianti
San Casciano Val di Pesa (FI) 50020, Italy
tel: (055) 8244288; fax: (055) 8244283
10 apartments
Lire 200,000 double B&B
3-day minimum stay-weekly stay preferred
Breakfast and occasional dinner
Open all year
Fluent English spoken
Region: Tuscany

A destination as special as the *maremma*, or southern Tuscany, can be kept secret for just so long. One response to increasing interest in its singular attractions is the opening or expansion of several noteworthy places to stay. The Villa Acquaviva, once owned by nobility, has been a small family hotel for the past seven years. The ambitious proprietors, Serafino and Valentina, completed extensive remodeling, to include seven guestrooms named for and painted in the colors of local wildflowers. The bedrooms all have private baths, and are decorated with country antiques and wrought-iron beds. The charming breakfast room has sky-blue tablecloths and looks out arched windows to a lush flower garden with alternating palms and umbrella pines, and on to a view over the gently rolling landscape up to the village of Montemerano—a quaint, medieval town with excellent restaurants and artisan shops. Breakfast of homemade cakes, breads and jams can be taken in or out on the patio. Just completed this year are eight additional rooms in a stone farmhouse on the property. These are our new favorites, with beautiful local antiques and colorful matching fabrics adorning beds and windows. The farmhouse has its own spacious breakfast room and living area downstairs. The hosts also produce both red and white wine, and olive oil, sold in their *Enoteca* shop on premises. *Directions:* From Rome, take the Aurelia road, exiting at Vulci. Follow signs for Manciano, then for Montemerano. Approximately 1-1/2 hours from Rome.

VILLA ACQUAVIVA
Hosts: Valentina Virginio & Serafino d'Ascenzi
Localita: Acquaviva
Montemerano (GR) 58050, Italy
tel & fax: (0564) 602890
15 rooms with private bathrooms
Lire 105-125,000 double B&B
3-day minimum stay in high season
Breakfast only
Closed February
English spoken well
Region: Tuscany

Another welcome addition to our B&B collection is the Fontanelle country house, sitting in the heart of the Maremma area of Tuscany. Besides being a pleasant and well-run B&B, it fills a need for the growing interest in this off-the-track destination. Signor Perna and his two lovely daughters, originally from Rome, searched and found this peaceful haven from the stress of city life, and promptly transferred themselves. Old black and white photographs adorn walls offering proof of the major restoration work put in several years ago. Looking over a soft green valley up to the nearby village of Montemerano, the family's contained stone farmhouse with its rusty red shutters, offers two comfortable rooms with spotless private bathrooms. The converted barn houses the remaining five rooms. Sunlight pours into the front veranda-like breakfast room where coffee and cakes are taken together with other guests at one large table. The Perna's assist guests in planning local itineraries including visits to artisan workshops. For those who prefer leaving their car behind, horses are saddled for competent riders who do not require a guide. *Directions:* From Rome, take A12 autostrada. Continue north on Aurelia rte 1, turning off at Vulci after Montalto. Follow signs for Manciano then Montemerano. Poderi is just a few km before town. Le Fontanelle is on the left.

LE FONTANELLE
Hosts: Daniela & Cristina Perna
Localita: Poderi di Montemerano
Montemerano (GR) 58050, Italy
tel: (0564) 602762
7 rooms with private bathrooms
Lire 110,000 double B&B
Breakfast only
Open all year
Some English spoken
Region: Tuscany

For four generations the Laudomia has been an immensely popular mealtime stop for day trippers in picturesque southern Tuscany, serving exquisite fresh-pasta dishes among other delicacies. So it made sense for Clara Casolaro and her daughter, Roberta, to add guestrooms so that visitors could linger and take full advantage of their warm hospitality. Son, Gianluca, following tradition, has just joined the staff. Once travelers discover this delightful combination of authentic regional cuisine, comfortable accommodations and unspoiled scenery, they become regulars. Rooms across the street from the restaurant all have private baths and are simply, but tastefully decorated with scattered antiques and bright floral bedspreads. The rooms off the roadside are quieter and offer lovely views across the rolling olive-tree-dotted hills. It is a memorable treat to dine in an intimate corner of the restaurant (filled with family antiques and artwork), especially if you put yourself completely in Clara's competent hands. A grape-arbor garden in back is a delightful spot to relax on a summer evening. In the vicinity are the thermal hot springs of Saturnia and many intriguing medieval towns, including Pitigliano, which seems carved out of the limestone cliff. *Directions:* From Rome, take the Aurelia road north, turning off at Vulci. Follow signs for Manciano, then Montemerano. From Siena, take the superstrada to Grosseto. Follow signs for Scansano, then Montemerano.

LOCANDA LAUDOMIA
Hosts: Clara Casolaro & family
Poderi di Montemerano (GR) 58050, Italy
tel: (0564) 620062 / 620013
12 rooms, 8 with private bathrooms
Lire 104,000 double B&B
  85,000 per person half board
3-day minimum stay
All meals served
Open all year
No English spoken
Region: Tuscany

Lucia Ana Luhan, whose parents are from Italy, grew up in a family rich in Italian tradition. She now lives in southern California, is married to a busy surgeon, has a family of three and operates several successful fresh pasta restaurants plus a catering service. Such activity would keep most women more than occupied, but not Lucia. While on holiday in Italy a few year ago, she fell in love with a 500-year-old stone farmhouse, bought it on a whim, and converted it into the Bed & Breakfast of Tuscany. Now Lucia commutes back and forth between California and Italy. When Lucia is not at her Italian farmhouse, it is well-managed by Renata Cerchiari who lives there all year. This seven bedroom inn is not luxurious, nor is it meant to be. All of the rooms are decorated in a homey, comfortable way; nothing contrived, just naturally pleasing and in keeping with the rustic nature of the old stone farmhouse. When the weather is mild, a bountiful breakfast is served outside on the terrace where guests congregate again in late afternoon to sip cool drinks while sharing their day's adventures. In the evening, if requested, a simple supper of homemade soup, cheeses and cold cuts is available. Or for guests who want a fancier dinner, the famous spa town of Montecatini is just a six-minute drive down the hill. New additions this year include a two-bedroom apartment, small swimming pool, cooking lessons, plus a "spa week." *Directions:* From Monsummano Terme (52 km east of Florence) drive 3 km northwest, following signs to Montevettolini.

BED & BREAKFAST OF TUSCANY
Hostess: Lucia Ann Luhan
Via dei Bronzodi 144
Montevettolini (PT) 51010, Italy
7 rooms, 6 with private bathrooms
1 apartment
tel & fax: (0572) 628817
$150 double B&B (USA)
Breakfast and dinner served
Open April 15-November 15
English spoken very well
Region: Tuscany

Novella and Laerte Piangatelli, delightful and gregarious hosts, have been welcoming guests into their home for over 10 years, ever since they moved to Emilia-Romangna from the south. Having agricultural experience, they were able to set up a farm, tended by Laerte, while Novella, the town schoolteacher, oversees the kitchen. She is an excellent cook and guests return time and time again for her pasta, joining the family at the long wood table in their rustic dining room with its hanging brass pots and ox harnesses. Guest accommodations have been transferred recently from upstairs in the white 18th-century farmhouse to the horse stalls, which have been converted into seven double rooms with private baths. The rooms are immaculate, if rather plain with basic modern furnishings. Guests tend to their own rooms and are even apt to help clear the table in the very informal and *en famille* atmosphere promoted at Le Radici. The sea, just 15 km away, can be seen in the distance, and several medieval towns and castles dot the hills in the surrounding countryside. A unique experience, best enjoyed if you speak some Italian. *Directions:* On route 9 from Rimini to Cesana, follow signs for Calisese and Montiano. Turn left at Esso gas station for Le Radici, or call for assistance.

LE RADICI
Hosts: Novella & Laerte Piangatelli
Localita: Montenovo
Via Golano 808
Montiano (OF) 47020, Italy
tel: (0547) 327001
7 rooms with private bathrooms
Lire 65,000 per person half board
Breakfast and dinner served
Open March-December
No English spoken
Region: Emilia-Romangna

In the northern Piedmont region, leading into the foothills of the Alps, is the peaceful countryside where Piercarlo Novarese, Il Mompolino's cordial host, decided to establish his inn and equestrian center. Run more like a small hotel, the sixteen guestrooms are divided between two mustard-color buildings. Each room has a private bath and balcony, and is complemented with rustic furnishings. The larger suites feature sitting rooms and are the nicest, furnished with the occasional antique. A large, open dining room serves breakfast, lunch and dinner, and boasts delectable regional dishes skillfully prepared by local women. Il Mompolino would make an ideal stopover on the way to the Alps, the lake region or Milan. It also provides an appealing spot to relax for a few days between more demanding tourist destinations. Sports activities abound, including horseback riding, tennis, swimming, and a gym with sauna. A variety of horseback-riding lessons is offered at the equestrian center, as are mounted excursions into the adjacent national park. Perhaps a good idea between bowls of pasta! *Directions:* Take the Carisio exit from the Milan-Turin A4 autostrada. From Carisio Mompolino is 7 km and well-marked.

IL MOMPOLINO
Host: Piercarlo Novarese
Mottalciata (VC) 13030, Italy
tel & fax: (0161) 857667
16 rooms with private bathrooms
2 apartments
Lire 90,000 double B&B
All meals served
Credit cards: all major
Open all year
Very little English spoken
Region: Piedmont

In a beautiful, unspoiled **area of northern** Umbria between the enchanting towns of Gubbio, Citta del Castello and Perugia, travelers are made to feel at home in the Berna family's hillside farmhouse on their 100-acre property. It is no wonder that the area, rich in Renaissance art and architecture, has become an international artist's colony, with frequent organized music festivals and art exhibits—the Bernas are natives of Rome. Three small stone houses clustered together make up the property, two for guests and one for Marisa and her family who come and go from the city. Stone walls, terra-cotta floors and beamed ceilings lend natural charm to the rooms, while lace curtains, handsome country antiques, floral sofas and dried flower arrangements enhance the cozy ambiance. Beautifully tiled bathrooms, living area and down-sized country kitchen are found in both houses, which are available for weekly rental only. In addition to being a gracious hostess, Marisa is actively involved in the community's cultural affairs and is an invaluable resource for information about the region. She also conducts week-long combination cooking and touring classes. *Directions:* From Perugia take route N3, exiting at Umbertide. Follow signs for Niccone and turn left in town towards Mercatale. Turn right up the hill after 3 km, or better, call from town!

LA MARIDIANA
Hosts: Berna family
Niccone 173
Umbertide (PG) 06019, Italy
tel & fax: (075) 9303234
2 houses, 4 rooms
Lire 150,000 double B&B
 90,000 per person half board
3-day minimum stay, Weekly preferred
Open all year
English spoken very well
Region: Umbria

On the border of Umbria and the Marches regions, within reach of the unforgettably romantic towns of Spoleto, Todi, Assisi and Perugia, is the 18th-century stone farmhouse of Francesco Rambotti. The house is beautifully situated atop a hill overlooking the peaceful countryside. Aside from wine-producing grapes, the farm raises deer, sheep and mountain goats, which roam freely on the property. Open for all meals, the tavern-like dining room has a fireplace, exposed-beamed ceiling, long wood tables and walls lined with wine casks. Hearty regional fare is served here, complemented by the farm's own wine. Guest accommodation is provided in the house with four double rooms sharing two baths, or alternately, two, two-bedroom apartments with bath and kitchenette. The furnishings are spartan and utilitarian, and the baths are new and immaculate. They are now producing natural creams and cosmetics at the farm using soil which is said to have been used in ancient times. The Rambotti family also owns another hotel (the Fontemaggio) in Assisi, whose restaurant is a popular local gathering spot. This part of the country is loaded with must-see destinations, and La Valle offers an inexpensive base from which to explore this incomparable area. *Directions:* From the Spoleto-Foligno road, turn right at La Valle 7 km after the town of Nocera.

LA VALLE
Host: Francesco Rambotti
Localita: Colle
Nocera Umbra (PG) 06020, Italy
tel: (0742) 810329; fax: (075) 912222
4 rooms sharing 2 bathrooms, 2 apartments
Lire 60,000-80,000 double B&B
* 40,000-55,000 per person half board*
All meals served
Open all year
Very little English spoken
Region: Umbria

It was a great pleasure to find such an attractive B&B spot so close to Orvieto, a fascinating and popular tourist destination, famous for its magical cathedral. The very cordial Belcapo family actually owns two adjacent farms on the outskirts and overlooking the majestic town on its limestone perch. La Cacciata also commands a dramatic view of the rich Umbrian valley below. The 200-acre farm/vineyard, in competent Belcapo-family hands for five generations, produces top-rated *Orvieto Classico* on a large scale, as well as a red and a rosé wine. The primary turn-of-the-century villa and one small stone house are reserved for family residences, while four other houses scattered around the property have been remodeled to accommodate guests. In the fifteen rooms, all but two with private bathrooms, care has been taken to preserve authentic architectural features and to select refined country antiques which blend harmoniously with them. An airy dining room overlooking the countryside and horse stables serves up sumptuous dinners. A swimming pool has just been added looking up to picturesque Orvieto, and horses are available for lessons or scenic outings. *Directions:* Exit from autostrada at Orvieto and turn left at the first stoplight on Viale 1 Maggio; follow signs for Porano, and follow signs to La Cacciata.

FATTORIA LA CACCIATA
Hosts: Settimio Belcapo family
Localita: Canale, Via La Cacciata 4
Orvieto (TR) 05010, Italy
tel: (0763) 92881 / 300892; fax: (0763) 41373
15 rooms, 13 with private bathrooms
Lire 70,000 double B&B
* 65,000 per person half board*
Breakfast and dinner served
Open all year
Very little English spoken
Region: Umbria

A convenient stopover while heading either north or south along the main artery—A1 autostrada—is the Villa Ciconia inn. Located below the historical center of Orvieto, in the newer commercial outskirts, the property maintains its tranquil setting thanks to the fortress of trees protecting the 16th-century stone villa. The first floor includes reception area, breakfast room and two large high-ceilinged dining rooms. These latter, with their somber greystone fireplaces, tapestries, heavy dark wood beams and subdued-color frescoes depicting allegorical motifs and landscapes, give the place a medieval castle's aire. The nine bedrooms on the second floor, all with ensuite bathrooms, are appointed in appropriate style, with antique chests and iron-wrought beds and all the amenities of a three-star hotel. Most rooms are quiet and look out onto the woods behind the villa. There are also two enormous beamed sitting rooms on this floor for guests. The restaurant has a solid reputation for creating excellent Umbrian specialties. *Directions:* Exiting from the autostrada, turn right towards Orvieto and right again where marked Arezzo, Perugia, passing under the tollway. The Ciconia is just after the river on the left-hand side of the road.

VILLA CICONIA
Hosts: Petrangeli family
Via dei Tigli 69
Orvieto (TR) 05018, Italy
tel: (0763) 92982; fax: (0763) 90677
9 rooms with private bathrooms
Lire 170,000-190,000 double B&B
All meals served
Credit cards: AX, VS
Open all year
English spoken well
Region: Umbria

Lo Spagnulo gives us a good idea of how the *masseria* farms of Apulia functioned in the 1600s. They were self-sufficient agricultural production centers, described as "factories," which included the proprietors' villa, housing for farmers, common dining area, church, administrative offices, animal shelters and work areas. Cities were dependent on these large complexes for fresh produce, meat and cheese. The Spagnulo still cultivates animals, fresh produce, almonds and olives. Fortress-like in appearance, its white-stone exterior leads inside to a courtyard garden, off of which the guest quarters are located. These vary in size and shape, many comprising two or three bedrooms, living/eating area and kitchen. Featuring the vaulted ceilings, exposed beams, terra-cotta floors and stone walls of the original building. The rooms display charm despite the somewhat spartan furnishings. These accommodations are recommended over the nondescript rooms which have been added in a modern building nearby. The stalls have been converted into a restaurant for guests serving typical local dishes family style. Proprietor Livino Massari, a professor, and his family are present on weekends and during the summer. *Directions:* Heading south on Route 379, exit at Marina di Ostuni. Follow signs to Rosa Marina, turning left at the sign for the farm.

MASSERIA LO SPAGNULO
Host: Livino Massari
Localita: Rosa Marina-Contrada Spagnulo
Ostuni (BR) 72017, Italy
tel: (0831) 970209; fax: (0831) 333756
25 apartments
Lire 80,000 double B&B
* 55,000 per person half board*
All meals served
Credit cards: AX, VS
Open all year
English spoken well
Region: Apulia

Paciano, situated on the border of Umbria and Tuscany, south of Lake Trasimeno, is an intriguing medieval village, perfectly intact, which was recently named the most ideal village in Italy. This has been reconfirmed by Greenpeace founder, David McTaggart, who retired to Paciano for its rich nature, and utter tranquillity. It is here where father and son team Giuseppe and Luigi Buitoni, of the famous family of pasta producers, decided to put to use their refined culinary skills. The old olive oil press, part of the family's 12th-century residence in the village, now functions as a restaurant with summer garden and B&B on the upper floors. Seven lovely bedrooms are decorated in refined country style, each with its own color scheme noted in the rich fabrics used for bedspreads and curtains. The palazzo was meticulously restored preserving all original architectural features. What are now closets were arched doorways, and the enormously high ceilings allowed for an extra floor to be incorporated. The upstairs breakfast and sitting room is soft and inviting with splendid antiques, floral tapestry armchairs, fresh flowers and crystal bottles lining shelves. A full buffet breakfast is served. *Directions:* Exit at Chiusi-Chianciano from the A1 autostrada; take road towards Trasimeno and Perugia and turn right up to town of Paciano where indicated.

LOCANDA DELLA ROCCA
Hosts: Buitoni family
Viale Roma 4
Paciano (PG) 06060, Italy
tel: (075) 830236; fax: (075) 830155
7 rooms with private bathrooms
Lire 130,000 double B&B
All meals served
Credit cards: AX, VS
Open: March-December
English spoken well
Region: Umbria

It was in 1987 when Rosemarie and Filippo bought and restored the elegant 16th-century Villa Montesolare (sun-colored as its name implies), opening its doors just recently to guests. Crowning a summit in unspoiled countryside (on one side—the approach side has been bombarded with new construction, invisible from the villa) between Umbria and Tuscany, just south of lovely Lake Trasimeno, the villa overlooks its surrounding estate cultivated with olive trees and grape vines. A wide gray-stone staircase leads up to the eight guestrooms and two suites, all with private bath and furnished in appropriate period style with carefully selected antiques. Across from the cozy bar at the entrance, where guests enjoy a cocktail together before dinner, is the intimate and elegant frescoed dining room, where fine Tuscan cuisine is presented under the supervision of Rosemarie. Guests are made to feel at home, whether relaxing in the impressive powder-blue upstairs salon with glass chandelier and massive stone fireplace, or wandering through the Italian Renaissance lemon-tree garden with corner chapel dating from 1500. Less passive activities include tennis, horseback riding, or swimming in the gorgeous hillside pool while awaiting an Umbrian sunset. *Directions:* From Perugia take N220 toward Citta di Pieve. After Fontignano (3 km), turn right at San Paolo which leads up to the villa.

VILLA DI MONTESOLARE
Hosts: Rosemarie & Filippo Strunk Iannarone
Localita: Colle San Paolo
Panicale (PG) 06064, Italy
tel: (075) 832376; fax: (075) 8355462
8 rooms and 2 suites with private bathrooms
Lire 109,000-126,000 per person half board
Breakfast and dinner served
Credit cards: VS, DC, MC
Open March-October
English spoken very well
Region: Umbria

Lovers of Tuscany's romantic countryside will envy the McCobbs, who after years in Rome decided to buy and restore an old stone farmhouse south of Siena and make a new home there. On the approach, at the crest of the dramatic cypress-lined drive, the visitor is rewarded with 360-degree view of the soft, green hills dotted with villages. The panorama should be appreciated upon arrival as you'll likely have trouble tearing yourself away from the luxurious comfort of the spacious guest quarters and refreshing swimming pool. The four suites consist of a cozy sitting area, fireplace, writing desk, library, and amenities such as refrigerator, phone and complimentary wine. The decor is a harmonious mix of antiques and family memorabilia (acquired through their world travels) which blend perfectly with the pretty floral-chintz upholstery and color-coordinated sheets. The palatial bathrooms are worth special mention since they provide so many decadent extras: whirlpool bath, his/her marble sinks, bathrobes and plush towels. Fresh muffins and breads are served either in the atrium breakfast room or out on the terrace. *Directions:* From Rome take the A1 autostrada, exiting at Chiusi. After Montepulciano, follow signs for Pienza. After 6 km watch for a small sign on the left indicating La Saracina.

LA SARACINA
Hosts: Jess & Don McCobb
Strada Statale 146, km 29.7
Pienza (SI) 53026, Italy
tel. & fax: (0578) 748022
4 suites, 1 room with private bathrooms
Lire 280,000 double B&B
Breakfast only
Open all year, weekends only January-February
Fluent English spoken
Region: Tuscany

Forty-five km northeast of Florence, in a beautiful, hilly area of Tuscany, is the Rufina valley, famous for the robust red wine of the same name. Crowning a wooded slope, is one of the many residences of the noble Galeotti-Ottieri family. The 15th-century main villa, where the family lives when not in Florence, was once a convent. The interior reveals spacious high-ceilinged halls with frescoes depicting family history. The family is also in the process of restoring several stone farmhouses on the vast property, one of which is the Locanda Praticino, whose upper floor contains eight lovely and simple double rooms, each with private bath and named after the color scheme they display. Downstairs is found a large dining and living room with vaulted ceiling, enormous stone fireplace and family antiques. A unique loft bedroom in the third-floor cupola offers a sweeping view of the lush countryside. Available for longer stays are five very tastefully decorated apartments (two in the main house). The Petrognano is a tranquil spot where guests may enjoy the gracious hospitality of a family whose ancestors played an important role in Florentine history. *Directions:* From Florence head toward Pontassieve. Continue to Rufina, turning right at Castiglioni-Pomino. The farm is just before Pomino

FATTORIA PETROGNANO
Hostess: Cecilia Galeotti Ottieri
Localita: Pomino
Rufina (FI) 50060, Italy
tel: (055) 8318812 or 8318867
8 rooms with private bathrooms
5 apartments
Lire 80,000 double B&B
All meals served
Open March-October
Little English spoken
Region: Tuscany

Elena and Cesare Taticchi heartily welcome guests to their tobacco and horse-breeding farm above Perugia. The roadside approach to this rambling renaissance villa is deceptive, as its beauty faces inward to the interior garden. The former stables near the main house contain a breakfast room and eight guestrooms with wood-beamed ceilings, brick floors and are sweetly furnished in simple country style. Ceramic bathroom tile (and lamps), handmade by their talented daughter, depict horses, ducks, roses, butterflies and the like, for which the rooms are named. The main villa's dramatic entrance foyer with arched stairway leads up to a glassed-in veranda overlooking a lush flower garden and woods through which the Tiber River flows. Elena serves her specialties in the elegant old-style dining room with chandelier and frescoes. Time stands still in the wonderfully cluttered library/billiard room, as well as in the two living rooms with grand piano, oriental carpets and period paintings. Twenty horses are available for lessons in the indoor/outdoor ring or excursions in the area. *Directions:* Take route E45 from Perugia and exit at Ponte Pattoli. Turn right at "T" intersection and continue for 1 km. The farm is just after tennis/sport complex (open to B&B guests).

IL COVONE
Hosts: Elena & Cesare Taticchi
Strada della Fratticiola 2
Ponte Pattoli (PG) 06085, Italy
tel: (075) 694140; fax: (075) 694503
8 rooms, 6 with private bathrooms
Lire 110,000 double B&B
  90,000-110,000 per person half board
3-day minimum stay
Breakfast and dinner served
Credit cards: all major
Open all year
Very little English spoken
Region: Umbria

The Vecchio Convento is a real gem, offering quality accommodation for a moderate price. Its several dining rooms are brimming with rustic country charm and serve delicious meals prepared from local produce. There are nine guest rooms, each with a private bathroom and tastefully decorated with antiques. The town of Portico di Romagna is like the inn, inviting yet unpretentious—an old village surrounded by wooded hills and clear mountain streams. A stroll through medieval pathways that twist down between the weathered stone houses leads you to an ancient stone bridge gracefully arching over a rushing stream. The inn too is old, and it was not (as you might expect given its name) originally a convent. According to its gracious owner, Marisa Raggi, it was named for a restaurant located in a convent that she and her husband, Giovanni (the chef), used to operate. When they moved here they kept the original name. The restaurant (closed Wednesdays) is still their primary focus, as its fine, fresh cuisine reflects. Due to the winding, two-lane mountain highway which leads to the village, it takes about two hours to drive the 75 km from Florence, but if you enjoy the adventure of exploring Italy's back roads, this small hotel will certainly become one of your favorites. *Directions:* The inn is located 34 km southwest of the town of Forli.

ALBERGO AL VECCHIO CONVENTO
Hosts: Marisa Raggi & Giovanni Cameli
Via Roma 7
Portico di Romagna (FO) 47010, Italy
tel: (0543) 967752; fax: (0543) 967877
20 rooms, 15 with private bathrooms
Lire 120,000 double B&B
All meals served (closed Wednesdays)
Credit cards: all major
Open all year
Some English spoken
Region: Emilia-Romagna

On the outskirts of historical Mantua is the Villa Schiarino, one of the magnificent estates formerly belonging to the Gonzaga family, once among the most powerful nobility in Lombardy. The cordial Lena Eliseo family, the present owners, have taken on the enormous task of restoring the 15th-century palace room by room. With high vaulted ceilings, completely frescoed rooms, wrought-iron chandeliers and original terra-cotta floors, the seemingly endless parade of rooms reveal one delight after another. Besides being a museum, the villa is also used for large parties, weddings, and business affairs. Surrounding the villa are small houses, once inhabited by farm hands, which are now available to travelers on a daily or weekly basis. The three modest, but spacious and comfortable apartments are appointed with a mixture of antique and contemporary furniture and can accommodate up to four persons. Each apartment has its own living area and one includes a kitchenette. This location is the ideal spot to base yourself while exploring less-touristy Ferrara, Cremona, Verona and Mantua, which are filled with medieval and renaissance buildings (Palazzo del Te and Palazzo Ducale are must-sees). *Directions:* From Mantua take route N62 past the church and turn left on Via Gramsci. Follow for 1 km to the villa.

VILLA SCHIARINO LENA
Hosts: Lena Eliseo family
Via Santa Maddalena 7
Porto Mantovano (MN) 46047, Italy
tel: (0376) 398238
3 apartments for 2-4 persons
Lire 70,000-100,000 daily per apartment
No meals served
Open all year
English spoken well
Region: Lombardy

High above the strip of shore holding the Fortino Napoleonico hotel sits the Hotel Emilia, owned by the Fiorini Dubbini family. Grandmother Emilia opened a small restaurant right on the beach 40 years ago, subsequently gaining an excellent reputation for fresh seafood dishes. That successful undertaking was succeeded by the hotel which, not surprisingly, has a restaurant known for seafood. It is surrounded by an extensive lawn sweeping to the edge of a cliff, where the vista drops 150 meters straight down to the sea below. Truly breathtaking views of Mount Conero and the dramatic, rugged coast, with its jagged rocky formations can be enjoyed from this point as well as from any of the guestrooms. The hotel itself is rather stark and modern with interiors softened by wicker couches topped by plump, yellow floral-print pillows, paintings and flower bouquets. This is a summer resort with swimming pool and tennis available on the premises, plus a nearby golf course. The all-white rooms are basic but comfortable with wicker and rattan beds and clean, tiled bathrooms. The cuisine, friendly hospitality, and unforgettable panoramas compensate for the somewhat spartan decor. *Directions:* Exit at Ancona Sud off autostrada A14 and follow signs for Camerano, then Portonuovo. Watch for signs indicating the entrance to the hotel.

HOTEL EMILIA
Hosts: Maurizio Fiorini family
Localita: Collina di Portonovo
Portonovo (AN) 60020, Italy
tel: (071) 801145; fax: (071) 801330
31 rooms with private bathrooms
6 apartments
Lire 150,000 double B&B
All meals served
Credit cards: all major
Open all year
English spoken well
Region: Marches

For those travelers wishing to explore the lesser-known Marches region, or about to embark on a ferry to Greece, the unique Fortino hotel offers comfortable and relaxing accommodations. Five km along the coast from the city of Ancona, the hotel boasts a beachfront location. Originally a fortress, the vantage point it affords must have been considered strategic by Napoleon in 1811, when he ordered it constructed. Fifteen guestrooms, three suites and a restaurant are housed within the low white, stone structure. The restaurant specializes in fresh seafood dishes and looks so directly out to sea, it gives the impression of being on a ship. At the heart of the fort is a courtyard, complete with cannons, where breakfast is served, and a separate building contains a bar and a spacious living room with fireplace, decorated in neoclassic style. Rich period antiques appoint the three lovely suites, while simpler wicker furniture is found in the double rooms. Just two steps away is the beach, and up on the roof of the one-story fort is a deck with a spectacular coastal view. A swimming pool is also available for guests. *Directions:* From Ancona, follow signs for Camerano. Take a left at Portonuovo, heading down to the sea. Watch for signs indicating the hotel's entrance.

FORTINO NAPOLEONICO
Hosts: Amleto Roscioni family
Portonovo (AN) 60020, Italy
tel: (071) 801125; fax: (071) 801314
30 rooms and 4 suites with private bathrooms.
Lire 200,000 double B&B
All meals served
Credit cards: all major
Open all year
English spoken well
Region: Marches

Accommodation of all levels is available in Positano's many hotels: from five-star luxury to simple bed and breakfasts. Casa Cosenza, with its sunny yellow facade, fits into the latter category. Sitting snug against the cliff side, halfway down to the beach, it is reached by descending one of the variety of stairways found in this unique seaside town. The front arched entranceway, lined with terra-cotta pots overflowing with colorful local flora, leads to an enormous tiled terrace overlooking the pastel-color houses of Positano and the dramatic coastline. Seven guestrooms on the second floor, each with private bathroom, enjoy the same breathtaking panorama. The residence dates back 200 years, as evidenced by the typical cupola ceilings in each room, originally designed to keep rooms cool and airy. Rooms have bright, tiled floors and are simply and sweetly decorated with old-fashioned armoires, desks and beds. Room 7, although with an older bathroom, has a lovely large terrace. The helpful and very friendly Cosenza family assures visitors a pleasant stay. *Directions:* It is best to park your car in a garage in town and ask for directions for the *scalinatella* stairway where there are signs to Casa Cosenza. Hopefully you will have packed light!

CASA COSENZA
Hosts: Cosenza family
Positano (SA) 84017, Italy
tel: (089) 875063
7 rooms with private bathrooms
Lire 100,000-120,000 double
No meals served
Open all year
Very little English spoken
Region: Campania

The spectacular Amalfi Coast is a stranger to agritourism, and there isn't a plethora of bed-and-breakfast-like accommodations, so the Fenice is a real find. The place is as fantastic as the mythological bird for which it is named. Guests leave their cars on the main road from Positano and climb the arbored steps to discover the idyllic white villa hidden amid the lush Mediterranean vegetation. The incredibly hospitable, young proprietors, Constantino and Angela and their two amusing sons, Giulio and Giacomo, welcome new arrivals on the shady front terrace, where each clement morning breakfast is served, accompanied by classical music. Six spacious bedrooms, each with spotless bath and a terrace with sea views that will leave you breathless are situated in one wing of the family's antique-filled home. Seven more rooms with balconies, reached by *many* steps down from the road, are built separately into the side of the cliff and have colorful, tiled floors and similar furnishings. Descending yet *more* steps (always surrounded by incredible coastal views), you'll come across the curved sea water pool and jacuzzi carved against the rock, where a fresh Mediterranean lunch is served at one big table, prepared primarily with ingredients grown on the premises. Constantino also attends to the olive-oil and wine production. This property is a natural wonder, cascading down to the sea and a small private beach. Our readers cannot seem to send us enough rave reviews about this place! *Directions:* Located on the coastal highway south of Positano in the direction of Amalfi, two curves after the town.

LA FENICE
Hosts: Constantino & Angela Mandara
Via Marconi 4
Positano (SA) 84017, Italy
tel: (089) 875513
15 rooms with private bathrooms
Lire 140,000 double B&B
Breakfast and lunch served
Open all year
Very little English spoken
Region: Campania

The Villa Rucellai rates high among Italian bed and breakfasts, due to its setting, style and gracious proprietors, the Rucellai Pique family. From the moment you enter the grand foyer looking out over the classical Italian Renaissance garden of this 16th-century country villa, all sense of time and place is lost. The Rucellai's devotion to their "farm" (in the family since 1759) is apparent, as is their warm and enthusiastic hospitality. Guests are given the run of the charming old home: from the cozy bedrooms, antique-filled library and spacious living room with fireplace, plump floral sofas and family portraits to the country kitchen and breakfast room overlooking a 14th-century pool, where guests are served *en famille* at a long wooden table. Members of the family enjoy suggesting itineraries of particular interest for their guests, as well as cultural events such as art courses, concerts and art exhibits. The Villa Rucellai provides truly special accommodation as well as serving as an excellent base from which to visit Florence (30 km), Siena (90 km), Lucca and Pisa. *Directions:* From Florence take the A11 autostrada, exiting at Prato Est. Turn right on Viale della Repubblica, then left on Borgo Valsugana, following signs for Trattoria La Fontana, and proceed on Via di Canneto for 2 km up to the Villa.

VILLA RUCELLAI DI CANNETO
Hosts: Giovanna Rucellai Pique family
Via di Canneto 16
Prato (FI) 50047, Italy
tel & fax: (0574) 460392 or 464986
11 rooms, 9 with private bathrooms
Lire 120,000 double B&B
Breakfast only
Open all year
Fluent English spoken
Region: Tuscany

One option (among at least 20 possibilities) for in-home accommodations in the Radda area is at the home of a gregarious Florentine couple, Giuliana and Enis Vergelli. On a long, winding road, just before the castle/village of Volpaia, is their stone house. The guest quarters are actually found in another stone house a few steps away in the quaint 14th-century village. The wood-shuttered residence can be rented entirely or as two separate apartments. One apartment is just like a doll house, comprised of a mini living area with minuscule fireplace, kitchenette and a ladder staircase leading up to the bedroom and bath; an absolutely adorable love nest for two. The other apartment, also on two floors, has a good-sized living room with kitchen, bathroom and two bedrooms, simply and very comfortably furnished. Guests are welcome to wander through the Vergelli's garden and enjoy the terrace with sweeping views over Chianti country. Giuliana adores pampering her guests and appears now and then with jams, honey or a freshly made soup. *Directions:* Driving through the town of Radda, turn right at signs for Volpaia castle. Follow uphill for several km to the first house before entering town, marked Vergelli.

AZIENDA AGRICOLA VERGELLI
Hosts: Enis & Giuliana Vergelli
Localita: Volpaia
Radda in Chianti (SI) 53017, Italy
tel: (0577) 738382
2 apartments
$400.00 (U.S.) weekly for 2 persons
$550.00 (U.S.) weekly for 4 persons
No meals served
Open all year
No English spoken
Region: Tuscany

Positioned atop a hill in the very heart of the Chianti region, sits Castelvecchi, a stone village rich in history dating back to the Middle Ages. Son Giovanni Catania runs the family's wine estate there with great vivacity and the pride that comes with cultivating land that has been in his family for 300 years. Today the estate is completely and faithfully restored. The eight double rooms are located in the 18th-century villa, while the five apartments (available for weekly stays) are found in surrounding stone buildings, originally dwellings for the farm hands. The rooms, each given the name of a native flower, are complete with all amenities, new bathrooms, good antique reproductions, wrought-iron beds and ornate chandeliers. A continental breakfast (or full upon request) is served in a large, bright room with a terrace. A round swimming pool and extensive garden make up the front yard of the villa, and offer an enticing spot to relax. This is an excellent base to explore the many captivating corners of Chianti from and learn more about the hundreds of varieties of its famous wine. *Directions:* Castelvecchi is exactly halfway between Florence and Siena. From Siena follow signs for Castellina in Chianti, then Radda. Castelvecchi is just north of town and is well-marked. From Florence, either take the Chianti road (longer but extremely scenic) to Greve, Panzano and Castelvecchi; or take Tavernelle exit from the Florence-Siena superstrada.

FATTORIA CASTELVECCHI
Hosts: Catania family
Radda in Chianti (SI) 53017, Italy
tel: (0577) 738050; fax: (0577) 738608
8 rooms with private bathrooms
14 apartments
Lire 100,000 double B&B
Breakfast only
Open all year
English spoken well
Region: Tuscany

Another addition to the group of house rentals in Radda is Le Selve, owned by a young couple who transferred to this serene countryside from Milan a few years ago. Their stone farmhouse is perched on a hilltop dominating the sweeping lush green landscape below—a truly heavenly 360 degree panorama. Sonia and Nando divided the house in three sections; one for themselves and their son, and two for their guests. The downstairs apartment has a bedroom, bathroom and living room with kitchenette and eating area. Upstairs is a larger apartment with the same characteristics plus a terrace which enjoys the best view. Both are furnished very simply and have fully-equipped kitchens for independent travelers. Sonia's great passion for horses has her spending most of her time down at the stables, where outings in the gorgeous countryside are organized. *Directions:* Coming from the west, just before Radda, turn right for San Sano and follow road until the sign S. Giusto in Salcio and turn right up hill to the farmhouse.

LE SELVE II
Hosts: Sonia & Nando Danieli
Localita: Le Selve-San Giusto
Radda in Chianti (SI) 53017, Italy
tel: (0577) 738196
2 apartments
$400.00 (U.S.) weekly for 2 persons
No meals served
Open all year
Some English spoken
Region: Tuscany

For its combination of idyllic location, charming ambiance and delightful hosts, the Podere Terreno is an example of the best in Italian bed and breakfasts. Sylvie and Roberto, a Franco-Italian couple, dedicate their lives to pampering their guests and seem to get as much enjoyment out of it as their guests do. The 400-year-old house is surrounded by terra-cotta flower vases, a grapevine-covered pergola, a small lake, and sweeping panoramas of the Chianti countryside. Within are seven sweet double bedrooms with bath, each decorated differently with country antiques and the family's personal possessions; a wine cellar loaded with the proprietors' own Chianti Classico; and a billiard room/library. Guests convene in the main room of the house around the massive stone fire-place on fluffy floral sofas for hors d'oeuvres and conversation, before sitting down to a sumptuous candlelit dinner, prepared completely by your hosts. Between courses, one's eye naturally wanders about the cozy, stone-walled room, filled with country antiques, brass pots and dried-flower bouquets hanging from the exposed beams, and shelves lined with bottles of wine—absolutely delightful. *Directions:* Leaving Radda, follow signs for Firenze, after 3 km turn right at Volpaia. After 5 km, turn right at sign for Podere Terreno.

PODERE TERRENO
Hosts: Sylvie Haniez & Roberto Melosi
Via della Volpaia
Radda in Chianti (SI) 53017, Italy
tel & fax: (0577) 738312
7 rooms with private bathrooms
Lire 140,000 double B&B
  110,000 per person half board
2-day minimum stay
Breakfast and dinner served
Credit cards: VS,MC
Open all year
English spoken very well
Region: Tuscany

Both Radda and Greve are excellent bases from which to explore scenic Chianti wine country with its regal castles and stone villages, in addition to Siena, Florence and San Gimignano. Radda in particular offers a myriad of possibilities for accommodation, including private homes whose owners have coordinated a booking service, in the case space is not available at one, similar arrangements can be made elsewhere. The Val delle Corti is the home and vineyard estate of the ex-mayor of Radda, Giorgio Bianchi (who runs the booking service) and his lovely wife, Eli. The cozy pale-stone house with white shutters tops a hill overlooking town. The hosts, who moved here 20 years ago from Milan, are extremely active in community affairs and are a superb source for area information. They offer guests a quarter of their home: a comfortable two-bedroom apartment with a separate entrance, a large bathroom, kitchen with all necessities, and living room with fireplace, all furnished simply with family belongings. On request, Eli will supply coffee and jam for the weekly stay, while others meals can be taken at their nephew's newly opened restaurant in town, *Le Vigne. Directions:* Equi-distant from Florence and Siena off the N222 Chianti road. Before entering Radda, turn right toward Lecchi-San Sano, then take first left at Val delle Corti.

PODERE VAL DELLE CORTI
Hosts: Eli & Giorgio Bianchi
Localita: La Croce
Radda in Chianti (SI) 53017, Italy
tel & fax: (0577) 738215
1 apartment
$550.00 (U.S.) per week
Half-board available at Le Vigne restaurant
Open Easter-October
English spoken very well
Region: Tuscany

On the opposite side of town from the Podere Val delle Corti (see preceding page), live Giorgio Bianchi's sister and family, who offer a two-bedroom apartment in a stone tower dating from 1832. This unique accommodation, perfect for a family of four, has an enchanting view of Radda and the countryside. The three-story tower has wood floors and beamed ceilings, a living room/kitchenette on the ground floor, one bedroom and a bath on the second floor, and a second bedroom on top. Furnishings are simple and in keeping with tower's rustic features. A small olive grove separates the tower from the Vitali's lovely home, where a swimming pool awaits road-weary guests. Lele is a vivacious hostess who divides her time between guests; a small in-house weaving business; and helping out her son and daughter-in-law, a young and ambitious couple who converted a farmhouse into the most authentic regional restaurant in town—*Le Vigne*. A half-board meal plan can be arranged for guests of the tower. *Directions:* From either Siena or Florence, follow signs for Radda off the spectacular *Strada del Chianti* N222. Go through town until you reach the hotel/restaurant Villa Miranda (not recommended), after which turn right at sign for Canvalle and follow dirt road up to the tower.

TORRE CANVALLE
Hosts: General & Lele Bianchi Vitali
Localita: La Villa
Radda in Chianti (SI) 53017, Italy
tel: (0577) 738321
1 apartment
$550.00 (U.S.) weekly, $620.00 (July & August)
Half board available at Le Vigne restaurant
Open Easter-November
English spoken very well
Region: Tuscany

The southeast corner of Tuscany is yet another delightful discovery for those who seek the road less traveled. From the Amiata mountains for nature lovers, to the hilltowns of Montepulciano, Pienza, Montalcino for wine and art lovers, to Chianciano and Vignoni for thermal baths, this area offers a rich variety of sites to explore. La Palazzina serves as the perfect base from which to visit these treasures. Adoringly run by mother and daughter team, Bianca and Nicoletta—one creates in the kitchen while the other tends to the guests. The restaurant is very special indeed. All the freshest, most natural ingredients from the farm are used in dishes whose recipes originate from the Renaissance period. The refined meals, highly rated by both *Michelin* and *Espresso* guides, are served in two elegant dining rooms, accompanied by Baroque music. The unusual checked tiled floors throughout the villa give it a cool, clean look and mix well with the many antique pieces. The 12 dainty bedrooms with immaculate bathrooms have been given women's names, each having its own color scheme. A swimming pool hugs the side of a hill overlooking the sweeping valley. *Directions:* From Florence on A1 autostrada, exit Chiusi and follow for Sarteano on rte 478, turning left before Radicofani for La Palazzina.

LA PALAZZINA
Hosts: Innocenti family
Localita: La Palazzina
Radicofani (SI) 53040, Italy
tel: (0578) 55771; fax: (0578) 53553
12 rooms with private bathrooms
3 apartments for 4 persons
Lire 84,000 per person half board
All meals served
Open April-October
Some English spoken
Region: Tuscany

Located in the far right-hand corner of the Chianti region is the Cortille farm, lovingly run by Florentine native Irene Gargani and her daughter's family. From its hilltop vantage point, the 16th-century, rustic stone farmhouse enjoys sweeping panoramic views of the countryside; as far as Siena on one side, and overlooking the picture-perfect stone village of Rapale on the other. The Gargani's wine production provides their primary livelihood. Two guestrooms, each with its own private bath, are located upstairs in the farmhouse, alongside the family quarters. The ambiance is very cozy and nostalgic, the rooms nicely cluttered with what may well be grandmother's antique country furniture, family photographs, lace curtains and portrait paintings. Guests dine together either in the beamed dining room with hanging brass pots or out on the cypress-lined patio overlooking the valley. Bordering Umbria, the Cortille is situated just an hour from Florence and equidistant to Siena, Arezzo, Cortona, Lago Trasimeno and Chianti. Its location makes it an ideal, and homey, base from which to readily explore these cultural treasures. *Directions:* From the A1 highway between Firenze-Arezzo, take the Valdarno exit. Follow signs for Montevarchi and Bucine, then take a left up to Rapale.

FATTORIA CORTILLE
Hosts: Irene Gargani & family
Localita: Rapale 10
Bucine (AR) 52020, Italy
tel: (055) 998000
2 rooms with private bathrooms
Lire 100,000 double B&B
* 85,000 per person half board*
Breakfast and dinner served
Open April-October
Some English spoken
Region: Tuscany

The Amalfi Coast has always been a favorite seaside escape for Italians and Americans (especially honeymooners), and Positano and Ravello are the cream of the resort areas. The best accommodations in Ravello are described in our other book on Italy, *Italian Country Inns & Itineraries*, however, the Villa Amore, a small family-run hotel is an economical alternative. It is ten minutes by foot from the main square in the direction of the romantic gardens of Villa Cimbrone. (Also not to be missed are the gardens of Villa Rufolo.) If you call from the main piazza, the hotel will send someone to collect your bags. A stone-walled path takes you to the simple hotel where a flight of stairs leads to the reception and sitting areas and the veranda restaurant surrounded by a flower garden. Here, high above the sea, guests are treated to one of the coast's more spectacular views. Several of the twelve rooms that friendly hostess, Ermerinda, offers, open out to this same garden with its potted geraniums and lounge chairs. Rooms with baths are rather basic, but are pleasant and clean. Local savory specialties, many of them seafood-based, are served either inside or out on the terrace looking down to the turquoise sea. *Directions:* From the square follow signs for Villa Cimbone, watching for Villa Amore, which is on the way.

VILLA AMORE
Host: Ermerinda Schiavo
Ravello (SA) 84010, Italy
tel & fax: (089) 857135
12 rooms with private bathrooms
Lire 85,000 double B&B
All meals served
Open all year
Little English spoken
Region: Campania

The Villa Maria is perhaps best known for its absolutely delightful terrace restaurant which has a bird's-eye view of the magnificent coast. Whereas most of Ravello's hotels capture the southern view, the Villa Maria features the equally lovely vista to the north. The Villa Maria is located two minutes by foot from the main square on the path winding to the Villa Cimbrone. After parking in the square (or at the Hotel Giordano), look for signs for the Villa Maria, which you'll find perched on the cliffs to your right. The building is a romantic old villa with a garden stretching to the side where tables and chairs are set, a favorite place to dine while enjoying the superb view. Inside, there is a cozy dining room overlooking the garden. The bedrooms are furnished with antique pieces including brass beds. The bathrooms have been freshly remodeled and some even have jacuzzi tubs. The hotel is owned by Vincenzo Palumbo whose staff speaks excellent English. Vincenzo also owns the nearby Hotel Giordano where there is a heated pool that you can use. You can expect a warm and gracious welcome at the Villa Maria, where guests are lucky enough to have the best of all worlds: a wonderful view and location in a charming villa with a fine restaurant. Directions: Ravello is about 6 km north of Amalfi on a small road heading north from highway.

VILLA MARIA
Host: Vincenzo Palumbo
Via San Chiara 2
84010 Ravello (SA) 84010, Italy
tel: (089) 857255; fax: (089) 857071
15 rooms with private bathrooms
2 apartments
Lire 160,000-180,000 double B&B
All meals served
Credit cards: all major
Open all year
English spoken very well
Region: Campania

Tuscany is the most visited region in Italy—mostly between Siena and Florence—but it nonetheless contains many other treasures off the beaten track. Heading west from Florence toward the coast are the lovely towns of Lucca and Pisa, and just north of them is the beautifully scenic area known as Garfagnana, which features two nature reserves and the Apuan Alps. Here in the northernmost tip of Tuscany is evidence of how Italian culture varies not only from one region to another, but within a region itself. In the heart of these mountains, the genial Coletti family runs a lively restaurant and cultivates cereals, wild berries and chestnuts. Just recently, the Colettis have added a B&B to their list of activities. Seven double rooms with a mountain-cabin feeling, pinewood floors and ceilings, have been fashioned in a restored three-story building in the stone village of Roggio. Most have a balcony and all have very nice modern bathrooms. Meals are taken around the corner at the family restaurant where Gemma Coletti prepares her special lasagna and polenta with porcini mushrooms, among other local specialties. Directions: From Lucca, take route 445 toward Castelnuovo and on to Roggio. Take a left up a winding road to Roggio, where a sign indicates the Da Gemma restaurant in the village.

AZIENDA COLETTI
Hosts: Gemma & Severino Coletti
Localita: Vagli Sotto
Roggio (LU) 55100, Italy
tel: (0583) 649179
7 rooms with private bathrooms
Lire 60,000 double B&B
All meals served
Open all year, except Christmas
Very little English spoken
Region: Tuscany

A delightful new addition to our group of accommodations in Rome is Casa Stefazio, the only true in-home B&B. Its location and setting is as perfect as the service and warm hospitality offered by Stefania and Orazio. The large, ivy-covered suburban home, just 30 minutes from the city center, is surrounded by several acres of manicured garden. Since their children have left the nest, the couple found themselves with four extra bedrooms, accessed by a separate entrance to the house. The B&B idea was the perfect solution. On the lower level are two bedrooms and one spacious "suite" accommodating a family of four, each with its own bathroom and each coordinating in its own color scheme. There is also a comfortable sitting area, plus sauna for guest use. On the first floor near the hosts' quarters is the fourth bedroom with own bathroom. The main areas include living room, unusually large American-style kitchen, where both Stefania and Orazio work wonders (he earned a Cordon Bleu diploma in his spare time), and eating area overlooking the expansive lawn and distant woods. Dinner is served on request under the pergola. Their style, in both decorating and easy entertaining, has obviously been influenced by their yearly trips to the States which they adore. Easily arranged, are sports activities such as horseback riding, tennis and swimming. Directions: Exit Settebagni from autostrada A1 and call to be met or given specific directions. With advance notice arrangements can be made to be picked up at the station or airport.

CASA STEFAZIO
Hosts: Stefania & Orazio Azzola
Via della Marcigliana 553
Rome 00138, Italy
tel & fax: (06) 87120042
4 rooms with private bathrooms
$120-160 (U.S.) double B&B
Breakfast only
Dinner served upon request
Open April-December
English spoken very well
Region: Lazio

The Hotel Cesari, just off the busy Via del Corso in the heart of the city, is a reputable hotel with a long-standing tradition of hospitality. The Cesari opened its doors over 200 years ago (in 1787) and has numbered among its guests such illustrious individuals as Stendhal, Garibaldi and Mazzini. Today, the hotel is efficiently run by the Palumbo family, with gracious daughter, Marina, taking charge. The hotel maintains a pleasant, old-world flavor, even if slightly worn around the edges. However, the fact that the establishment is slowly undergoing a facelift is reflected in the relatively low room rates charged by the proprietors, which make it a good value in an expensive city. A double salon decorated with plump red-leather armchairs, worn oriental carpets, period paintings and ornate chandeliers greets arriving visitors. The spacious guestrooms all include a private bath, and are simple and comfortable, with soft floral armchairs and older furnishings. Breakfast is served in the rooms, as there is no common dining area. The hotel staff were exceptionally courteous and helpful. Directions: Use a detailed city map to locate the hotel off the Via del Corso.

HOTEL CESARI
Hosts: Anna Palumbo family
Via di Pietra 89
Rome 00186, Italy
tel: (06) 6792386; fax: (06) 6790882
50 rooms, 40 with private bathrooms
Lire 200,000 double B&B
Breakfast only
Credit cards: all major
Open all year
English spoken well
Region: Lazio

The Due Torri is a perfect example of a small and charming city hotel, a breed not easy to find in today's urban centers. The building, dating to the early 1800s, is tucked away on a tiny, narrow street in the quiet historical section of Rome between the Spanish Steps and Navona Square. Renovated three years ago, the twenty six very small bedrooms are decorated with care and taste, featuring spotless bathrooms, period antiques and peach-colored fabric walls. Many amenities are offered, including elevator and air conditioning, which provides welcome (if not critical) relief on Roman hot summer days. The cozy and impressive reception, sitting area and breakfast room have oriental carpets, cream color draperies, gilt-framed mirrors and paintings, and elegant tapestry chairs. A rooftop terrace is currently being restored. A very friendly staff is eager to make suggestions for local sightseeing. Superbly located, Due Torri is a popular hotel, so be sure to reserve your room at least one month in advance. Directions: Use a detailed city map to locate the hotel, north of Navona square amidst a maze of winding streets.

HOTEL DUE TORRI
Hostess: Lidia Aperio Bella
Vicolo del Leonetto 23
Rome 00186, Italy
tel: (06) 68806956; fax: (06) 68865442
26 rooms with private bathrooms
Lire 200,000 double B&B
Breakfast only
Credit cards: all major
Open all year
English spoken well
Region: Lazio

Many hotels in Rome can boast panoramic views over the city, but few have such a close up view of a world-famous monument as the Fontana Hotel. Situated directly on the square containing the beautiful Trevi fountain, the Fontana's windows look out on to its gushing waters, where you can practically toss a coin from your room. The fountain has only recently been brought back to life following years of tedious restoration work, and is magnificent. The sleek black-and-white breakfast room doubles as a bar and is situated on the top floor of the 17th-century building, giving guests a bird's-eye view over the square from an enormous picture window. The twenty-seven rooms are sweetly done with pastel-floral wallpaper, bedspreads, and white curtains. Bathrooms were incorporated into each room later, and are therefore quite small. Vaulted ceilings crown the narrow halls leading to the guestrooms, and are adorned with antique prints of Rome. Signor Manlio and Signora Elena at the desk handily attend to guests' every need. The noise commonly associated with a city hotel is not a problem here as the square is closed to traffic although loud voices of tourists lingering into the early hours can be a problem in the summer months—the fountain closes at midnight. Directions: Use a detailed city map to locate hotel in the Piazza di Trevi off the Via Tritone.

FONTANA HOTEL
Hosts: Elena Daneo & Manlio Gazzabin
Piazza di Trevi 96
Rome 00187, Italy
tel: (06) 6786113 / 6791056
fax: (06) 6790024
24 rooms with private bathrooms
Lire 210,000 double B&B
Breakfast only
Credit cards: all major
Open all year
English spoken well
Region: Lazio

The Locarno Hotel is a wonderful option in the urban B&B category. Centrally located on the corner of a rather busy street, it is only two blocks from bustling Popolo Square. Its downtown location makes noise unavoidable, so it is advisable to request a room which is not over the street. The palazzo housing the Locarno dates back to the turn of the century, and the hotel itself opened in 1925. Even with the extensive renovations it has undergone, the establishment retains the art-deco flavor it had originally. The red-carpeted reception area leads to a cozy bar and long, mirrored sitting room lined with cushioned banquettes and cafe tables. There is also a side patio with shady canvas umbrellas where guests can take breakfast in warm weather, if not in the new and cheery breakfast room looking out to the patio. Another fabulous addition is the opening of the rooftop garden where one can take a break or study an itinerary while gazing over Rome's tiled roofs and terraces to St.Peter's dome and Villa Borghese park. The thirty-eight rooms with bathrooms are decorated with antiques, gold-framed mirrors and pretty floral wallpaper. The Locarno features such extras as a parking garage and free use of bright red bicycles with which you might tour the Villa Borghese park. It is no wonder that this is a favorite among artists and writers. Reserve well in advance. Directions: Use detailed city map to locate hotel one block east of the Tiber River at Flaminia square sign.

HOTEL LOCARNO
Hostess: Caterina Valente
Via della Penna 22
Rome 00186, Italy
tel: (06) 3610841; fax: (06) 3215249
38 rooms and 2 suites with private bathrooms
Lire 230,000 double B&B
Breakfast only
Credit cards: all major
Open all year
English spoken well
Region: Lazio

This small centrally located hotel gets its name, as you might guess, along with its relatively high prices, from its proximity to Rome's most famous square just three blocks away. The hotel has been in business since the 1920s and has just recently been renovated. The contained, mirrored reception and sitting area is divided by a sweeping red-carpeted stairway leading up to the twenty guestrooms found on three floors. The rooms are neat and clean, if somewhat uninspired, and feature private baths—two with jacuzzi—and simple, practical furnishings. The top-floor rooms also have small balconies lined with flowerpots. Breakfast can be arranged and served in rooms upon request, but it is not included in double rate. The cordial owners, Signor and Signora Giocondi, have been operating the hotel for the past 30 years, and are always present and happy to answer any questions. The hotel's location affords guests an easy walk to excellent restaurants and some of the most famous boutiques in the world. Directions: Use a detailed city map to locate hotel three blocks west of the Piazza di Spagna

HOTEL PIAZZA DI SPAGNA
Owner: Bernardino Giocondi family
Via Mario de'Fiori 61
Rome 00187, Italy
tel: (06) 6796412; fax: (06) 6790654
16 rooms with private bathrooms
Lire 220,000 double
No meals served
Credit cards: VS,MC
Open all year
Very little English spoken
Region: Lazio

Just north of the famous Navona Square with its marvelous Bernini fountains, is the small and centrally located Portoghesi Hotel in the oldest section of Rome. A landmark hotel, accommodation has been offered here for over 150 years, and every effort has been made to maintain an intimate, family-run atmosphere. The property was recently given a facelift, and now most rooms have new, private bathrooms plus air conditioning, telephone and TV. An elevator takes guests up to the guestrooms, which are decorated in two distinct styles: a clean and simple modern look or, as with the preferred corner rooms No. 8, 24 and 44, pleasant and modest with antique beds and armoires. Each floor has its own cozy sitting area with gilded mirrors, paintings and antique chairs. A pleasant extra is the rooftop terrace overlooking the terra-cotta roofs typical of Rome, as well as the cupola of the famous church after which the hotel and street are named. Breakfast is served on this arbored, outdoor terrace in the warmer months. Reserve at least one month in advance. Ask for a room off the street, as moped traffic can be noisy. Signor Mario and his sons attentively look after the needs of their guests. Directions: Use a detailed city map to locate the hotel in the heart of Rome.

HOTEL PORTOGHESI
Hosts: Mario & Marco Trivellone
Via dei Portoghesi 1
Rome 00186, Italy
tel: (06) 6864231; fax: (06) 6876976
26 rooms, 23 with private bathrooms
Lire 190,000 double B&B
Breakfast only
Credit cards: VS, MC
Open all year
English spoken well
Region: Lazio

The exceptionally priced Hotel Tea, situated just a few blocks from the internationally famous Via Veneto, lined with foreign embassies, boutiques and grand hotels, has been catering to embassy visitors for over thirty years. The turn-of-the-century building was originally the private residence of the Princess Tea until the Moioli and Devoti families bought it in 1960. Son, Mario, returned to Rome from the United States with his American wife, Anne, who gives a hearty welcome to guests at the front desk. Anne has enthusiastically tackled the ongoing task of giving the hotel a badly needed facelift. The thirty-five rooms, many with new bathrooms, each have a distinct personality, combining as they do a variety of floral-print wallpapers, wrought-iron beds, small sofas (that can be used as a third bed) and worn oriental carpets. There is a warm and pleasantly homey feeling to the place once you've gotten past the rather uninspired entrance. A favorite spot is the elegant high-ceiling living room with its pastel-blue fabric chairs, chandeliers, and enormous painted portrait, leftover from the days of Princess Tea. Downstairs is the paneled tavern breakfast room and another spacious lounge. Ask for a suite, which are priced the same as doubles. Directions: Use detailed city map to locate the hotel four blocks east of Via Veneto.

HOTEL TEA
Hosts: Giulio Moioli family
Via Sardegna 149
Rome 00187, Italy
tel: (06) 4885964; fax: (06) 4744243
35 rooms with private bathrooms
Lire 176,000 double B&B
Breakfast only
Credit cards: all major
Open all year
Fluent English spoken
Region: Lazio

The Teatro di Pompeo, a well-managed, efficient and friendly small hotel, gets its name from the ruins of the Pompeius Theater (55 BC) which were actually discovered under the building's foundation. The pale yellow hotel is centrally located between Navona Square and Campo dei Fiori Square, an area characterized by authentic local color and narrow streets lined with artisan's workshops. It is fast becoming the place to live in the city, and every other building has been restored and painted in the wonderful, faded earth tones so typical of Rome. Signor Luigi, at reception enthusiastically welcomes guests to the twelve new and spotless bedrooms, simply and tastefully decorated with antique prints of ancient Rome, and warmed overhead by original beamed ceilings. Many amenities, including air conditioning (supplemental charge), spotless bathrooms, TV and telephone are available in each room. Descending a short flight of stairs from the mini-reception and bar area brings you to the dark, cave-like breakfast room, unique in that it is part of the ancient Pompeian theater. Next door is the Der Pallaro restaurant, a favorite with the local citizenry, where guests can treat themselves to a genuine Roman meal. Directions: Use a detailed city map to locate hotel three blocks east of Campo dei Fiori square.

HOTEL TEATRO DI POMPEO
Host: Lorenzo Mignoni
Largo del Pallaro 8
Rome 00186, Italy
tel: (06) 68300170; fax: (06) 68805531
12 rooms with private bathrooms
Credit cards: all major
Lire 210,000 double B&B
Breakfast only
Open all year
English spoken well
Region: Lazio

Behind the city gates of Porta Pinciana, whose ancient walls lead from the Via Veneto, is tranquil, tree-lined Via Nomentana, once a luxurious residential street in this part of the city. Many elegant pastel-colored villas remain (including that of Mussolini), but the majority of them have been converted into embassy-owned apartments over the years. The Villa del Parco has been transformed into a lovely and quiet hotel with a B&B feel to it. A flower-edged driveway leads to the villa, passing by tables set up for breakfast in the small front garden. The sensation upon entering the pleasant lobby scattered with antiques and comfy sofas is that you've arrived home. Two cozy sitting rooms invite guests to sit and relax. The twenty-five guestrooms, each with private bath, are divided among the three floors of the hotel. Half of the bedrooms have been renovated and they all vary greatly in size and decor, which tends to be a mixture of old and new furnishings. Request one of the newer (and larger) rooms facing out the back of the hotel just in case the street noise might be disturbing. The Bernardini family and friendly staff are happy to make restaurant and itinerary suggestions and, as parking is always a problem, take note that a reputable garage (with limousine service) is located just across the street. Directions: Rely on a detailed city map to locate the hotel in a residential district- a 15 minute walk from the center of town.

HOTEL VILLA DEL PARCO
Hosts: Bernardini family
Via Nomentana 110
Rome 00161, Italy
tel: (06) 8554115; fax: (06) 8540410
25 rooms with private bathrooms
Lire 205,000 double B&B
Breakfast only
Credit cards: all major
Open all year
Some English spoken
Region: Lazio

Every place in Italy seems to be famous for some type of food or wine, and Parma is no exception, being without doubt the city most internationally known for its cheese and prosciutto, which you should not fail to sample while you're in the region. Thirty km from Parma are found the curative thermal waters of Salsomaggiore and just beyond town is the Antica Torre. The ancient 13th-century tower majestically crowns a hilltop overlooking the soft green countryside. The Pavesi family, proprietors of the surrounding farm, offer warm hospitality to its guests within the tower. One bedroom with bath is located on each of the tower's three floors and in addition, the family has a large two-bedroom apartment available in the main house, which would be ideal for a family. Rooms are simply decorated, and have lovely views over the valley. Three additional apartments have been recently incorporated. There is also a swimming pool and horseback riding. The barn has been converted into a pleasant dining room where fortunate guests sit down together to a hearty homemade meal, typically Emiliana in style, including fresh pastas, vegetables, meat and poultry directly from the farm. *Directions:* From Salsomaggiore, go through town, following signs for Cangelasio and Antica Torre.

ANTICA TORRE
Hosts: Francesco Pavesi family
Localita: Cangelasio-Case Bussandri 197
Salsomaggiore Terme (PR) 43039, Italy
tel: (0524) 575425
4 rooms with private bathrooms
4 apartments
Lire 90,000 double B&B
  60,000 per person half board
All meals served
Open April-November
Very little English spoken
Region: Emilia-Romagna

Though near both Verona and Lake Garda, the Ca'Verde farm feels miles away from civilization, immersed in a wooded valley in the Veneto wine country. Nine families got together 12 years ago to purchase the unusual stone Provence-style farmhouse, originally a 15th-century convent, and turned it into a busy dairy farm. Their idea was to save the historic building, the many acres of land around it, and create local employment by producing cheese and yogurt on the farm. They adhere to traditional production methods without additives or preservatives. Five attic rooms have been fashioned for guests in the enormous U-shaped house where three of the families live. Rooms are small and utilitarian, with rustic wood beds, beamed ceilings with skylights and one clean, modern bathroom for every two rooms. Three new more comfortable rooms with bathrooms have been added (at a slightly higher rate) to another wing. A main attraction is the *trattoria* specializing in regional recipes (fresh pasta and truffles, vegetarian dishes) and homemade wine, served in three informal dining rooms with red-checked tablecloths and large fireplaces. Guests dine in or out on the patio, and in the summer are treated to outdoor concerts and cinema. *Directions:* From Verona take the A12 autostrada toward Brennero. Exit at Verona Nord, and follow signs for San Ambrogio. Go through town and start up hill, watching for small sign for Ca'Verde on left hand side of road.

CA'VERDE
Host: Alessandro Lanza
Azienda Agricola 8 Marzo
San Ambrogio Valpolicella (VR) 37010, Italy
tel: (045) 6861760; fax: (045) 7731888
9 rooms, 4 with private bathrooms
Lire 58,000 double B&B
* 53,000 per person half board*
All meals served
Open March-December
Some English spoken
Region: Veneto

Agritourism and B&B-type accommodations are virtually non-existent in the northern lake district, so coming across the enchanting Villa Simplicitas was a special treat. The pale yellow country house of Milanese family Castelli, sits high up in the hills between Lakes Como and Lugano and is surrounded by thick woods. There is a wonderful old-fashioned charm to the place, enhanced by many heirloom turn-of-the-century antiques scattered about the cozy living and dining rooms. Pretty floral fabrics cover sofas and armchairs, in perfect harmony with the soft yellow walls bordered with stenciled designs. The same warmth is spread among the 10 guest bedrooms with their pinewood floors and *trompe l'oeil* paneled walls, antique beds and lace doilies adorning dressers. Innovative meals are prepared by chef Mantelli using his worldwide experience, and are served either in or out on the veranda with green and white striped awnings and matching director's chairs. In the evening, impeccably-set tables are candlelit for a romantic dinner for two—simply heavenly. *Directions:* From Como head north to Argegno. Turn left passing through S. Fedele, then left and continue up to S. Fedele. Just after town at the bus station, turn left—2 km up to the house.

VILLA SIMPLICITAS
Hosts: Curzio Castelli family
Localita: Simplicitas
San Fedele d'Intelvi (CO) 22028, Italy
tel: (031) 831132
10 rooms with private bathrooms
Lire 120,000 double B&B
All meals served
Open: April-October
English spoken well
Region: Lombard

Due to the ever-increasing popularity of the stunning medieval village of San Gimignano, accommodations in the surrounding countryside have flourished. La Casanova is a typical square stone farmhouse with wood shutters and red-tile roof, which you'll grow accustomed to seeing throughout Tuscany. The bed and breakfast's exceptional feature is that it enjoys a privileged view of the towers of San Gimignano, an ancient town referred to as the "Manhattan" of the year 1000. Marisa and Monica Cappellini are jovial hostesses who pride themselves on offering comfortable and immaculate accommodations to their international clientele. Breakfast is served on the outside patio where guests are immersed in breathtaking scenery, the first thing in the morning before heading out to visit intriguing San Gimignano and the many surrounding villages. This is an authentic and simple wine-producing farm with eight double rooms with private baths. Country furniture characteristic of the region decorates the rooms, whose original architectural features have been preserved. *Directions:* From San Gimignano take the road toward Volterra. After 2 km, turn left at the sign for *Casanova*, not Hotel Pescille.

CASANOVA DI PESCILLE
Hostess: Marisa Cappellini
Localita: Pescille
San Gimignano (SI) 53037, Italy
tel & fax: (0577) 941902
8 doubles with private bathrooms
Lire 90,000 double B&B
Breakfast only
Credit cards: VS, MC
Open all year
No English spoken (some French)
Region: Tuscany

Accidentally coming upon the Casolare, tucked away into the hills five miles beyond medieval San Gimignano, was a delightful surprise. Just before reaching the B&B, you'll see an abandoned stone convent dating back to 1100—leading your imagination wandering to the past. Leaving the convent and the tourists behind, guests arriving at the Casolare feel as if they're coming "home." The attractive renovated farmhouse, hosted by Berta and Andrea, a young antique dealer, retains all of the features characteristic of the original structure. The four double rooms with bath are extremely comfortable and reflect superb taste. The one suite for 2-4 persons with its own terrace and the common sitting room and dining room have been decorated with refined antiques as well. Guests receive a folder of watercolor prints by a local artist depicting the various sites in the area with a description of each on the back. The original paintings adorn an entire wall in the living room. An extra bonus is the lovely pool which provides refreshment and relaxation after a hot day sightseeing, while anticipating another appetizing meal at dusk, poolside. Berta is an excellent cook and prepares very special Tuscan menus. This is a truly tranquil spot. *Directions:* From San Gimignano follow signs for Montaione. Staying left at the fork, turn right onto dirt road for Libbiano and take to the end.

CASOLARE DI LIBBIANO
Hosts: Andrea & Berta Bucciarelli
Localita: Libbiano 3
San Gimignano (SI) 53037, Italy
tel & fax: (0577) 955102
4 rooms and 1 suite with private bathrooms
Lire 110,000 per person half board
3-day minimum stay
Breakfast and dinner served
Open Easter-October
Some English spoken
Region: Tuscany

The increasing popularity of this perfectly intact medieval town and the resulting availability of accommodations has made San Gimignano a hub from which tourists fan out to visit nearby, less-well-known treasures such as Volterra, Colle Val d'Elsa and Monteriggioni. A very pleasant stay is very likely at the Podere Villuzza, run by friendly young Sandra and Gianni Dei. Following restoration of their 150-year-old stone farmhouse, they opened the doors to guests five years ago. Chairs are set up in front where visitors can enjoy the view of vineyard-covered hills that lead up to the impressive multi-towered town. A hearty dinner may be shared with other guests in the simple country-style dining room where Sandra prepares tantalizing, fresh specialties from the family recipe book. Her husband occupies himself with the production of top-quality Vernaccia wine. Two double rooms with nice new bathrooms are upstairs, furnished with wrought-iron beds and antique armoires, complemented by mansard ceilings. The larger double has a private terrace overlooking the back hills. Also available are three small apartments within the house that include a living area and kitchen. *Directions:* Go through town and follow signs for Certaldo. After 2 km turn right and follow signs for Villuzza.

PODERE VILLUZZA
Hosts: Sandra & Gianni Dei
Strada 25
San Gimignano (SI) 53037, Italy
tel: (0577) 940585; fax: (0577) 942247
2 rooms and 3 suites with private bathrooms
Lire 87,000 double B&B
Breakfast and dinner served
Open all year
English spoken well
Region: Tuscany

In the heart of the wine valley of Piedmont, between the principal cities of Piedmont: Alessandria, Alba and Asti, is lovely and serene countryside characterized by rolling green hills lined with vineyards and a strong tradition of fine country dining. Maria and Piercarlo are a local couple who have dedicated their lives to their farm and its production of Barolo and Dolcetto wines, as did their parents and grandparents. In fact, their typical white rectangular farmhouse has been in the family for well over 100 years. Over those years, as the family grew, so did the main house, eventually being connected to the barn and stables to make room for everyone. A family of just three, the Carellis found themselves with extra space and decided to use two of the bedrooms for guests, leaving grandmother's simple antiques in them, and adding one spotless bathroom in between. The dining room is popular with locals, and will serve up an unforgettable meal of homemade tagliatelle, lamb and other regional specialties. Guests get a peek at a real farmer's lifestyle—some knowledge of Italian recommended. *Directions:* From San Marzano, take the road leading north from town toward Agliano, turning right at chapel and follow signs for the farm.

ANTICA FATTORIA DEL COLLE
Hosts: Maria & Piercarlo Carelli
Reg. Chierina 17
San Marzano Oliveto (AT) 14050, Italy
tel: (0141) 856252
2 rooms sharing 1 bathroom
Lire 75,000 per person full board only
All meals served
Open all year
No English spoken
Region: Piedmont

On the other side of town from the Antica Fattoria (see previous page) is another typical farmhouse and vineyard run cooperatively by several local families. Three simple and very neat bedrooms upstairs are available for guests, decorated with country furniture typical of the area. Two of the five bedrooms have ensuite bathrooms. The farm work seems to be evenly divided among these energetic families, whose members convene along with locals at lunch time in the spacious and rustic restaurant on the premises. Here they can count on a hearty full-course meal prepared from the freshest possible ingredients directly off their land. This provides a convenient and very economical location from which to launch excursions to some of the delightful villages in the immediate vicinity, and of course, to Alba and Asti, which should not be missed. You can also take shorter trips on horseback from nearby stables into the scenic surrounding countryside. Or alternatively, the Italian riviera lies just an hour and a half away. *Directions:* Coming from the direction of Nizza Monferrato, take the middle road at the triple fork just before San Marzano. La Viranda is just up the road on the left.

LA VIRANDA
Hostess: Lorella Solito
Localita: Corte 64
Piazza Martiri Liberta 2
San Marzano Oliveto (AT) 14042, Italy
tel: (0141) 856571
5 rooms, 2 with private bathroom
Lire 38,000 double B&B
* 30,000 per person half board*
All meals served
Closed August & January
Some English spoken
Region: Piedmont

The complex of stone houses known as Borgo Spante dates back to the 15th Century and has been in the same family since 1752. Consisting of a main villa, connecting farmers' houses, chapel, barns, swimming pool and garden, it is isolated in 500-acres of woods and hills, yet only 10 miles from Orvieto and not far from Assisi, Todi and Perugia. Daughter Claudia decided to move into the summer residence full time and run a B&B. She does a superb job of it. Guests stay in a combination of rooms and apartments in the former farmers' quarters, left intact with their irregular sized rooms, sloping worn-brick floors and rustic country furnishings—very charming in its way. Authentically Umbrian meals, prepared by local women, are served in the dining room with long wood tables and fireplace. A larger dining area has just been completed in the former barn, along with four additional mini-apartments—simply and characteristically decorated. Memorable evenings are spent in the garden or poolside conversing with other guests or listening to an impromptu concert. *Directions:* From the A1 autostrada exit at Orvieto and follow signs for Arezzo on route 71. After 7 km turn right at Morrano and proceed for 12 km until the sign for Spante. Turn left and continue for 2 km.

BORGO SPANTE
Hostess: Claudia Spatola
Localita: Ospedaletto
San Venanzo (TR) 05010, Italy
tel & fax: (075) 8709134, 8709272
5 rooms with private bathrooms
8 apartments
Lire 75,000 per person half board
2-day minimum stay
Breakfast and dinner served
Open all year
Some English spoken
Region: Umbria

In the olive-strewn countryside around the magical town of Ostuni is the Tenuta Deserto farm, where the Roman Lancelloti family has summered for centuries. This *masseria* was built in several periods dating back to the 1600s, and is made up of the main house, a chapel, a 16th-century stone tower and several houses which were once farmers' quarters. The main brick villa has been divided into sections—a large part reserved for a three-bedroom apartment with three bathrooms, fully equipped kitchen and living room. Four more two-and three-bedroom apartments have been created in outlying white houses, one being of actual *trullo* construction, with cone-shaped stone roof, typical of the Alberobello area. Young and gracious Sveva and Riccardo have been hosting travelers for 12 years and are most attentive to their needs. The spacious rooms are decorated with taste and care, using family antiques, botanical prints, local handicrafts and brightly colored floral bedspreads. Guests convene at poolside or in the lovely "clubhouse" living room with fireplace and vaulted ceilings. Meals can be arranged upon request. *Directions:* From Bari take the coastal route N379, exiting at San Vito. Cross through town, following signs for Ceglie. After 3.5 km turn right on dirt road at B&B sign.

TENUTA DESERTO
Hosts: Sveva & Riccardo Lancellotti Delfino
San Vito dei Normanni (BR) 72019, Italy
tel: (0831) 393062; fax: (06) 3219566
6 apartments
Lire 400,000-l,200,000 weekly
per apartment (2-7 people)
Weekly stay required in July & August
Dinner served upon request
Open April-October
English spoken very well
Region: Apulia

Right in the heart of the chic (and expensive) Italian riviera is a small jewel of a B&B, hugging the hillside above the ports of Portofino and Santa Margherita. With great determination, the young and handsome host, Roberto Gnocchi, decided to completely restore the small stone farmhouse on a piece of the family's property. Three tastefully decorated double rooms, each with private bath, are offered to guests, along with panoramic views over the fruit orchard and down to the sea. A cozy high-ceilinged living room, inviting one to curl up with a book or converse, gives visitors the feeling of being at the home of friends. The ambiance is intimate and welcoming. In the beamed dining room, breakfast and dinners (featuring local specialties) are served— often prepared by Roberto himself. To accommodate the increasing number of requests, four additional rooms have been created in the former private home next door, decorated in the same warm fashion with scattered antiques. From Genoa to the marvels of Cinque Terre, the Ligurian coast holds some very special treasures to discover, and the Gnocchi B&B makes a perfect and very reasonable place from which to discover them. *Directions:* From Santa Marghereta follow signs to Genova going uphill for about 4 km until you see a blue sign indicating an intersection. Just after, is a narrow road on the left with a gate.

GNOCCHI
Host: Roberto Gnocchi
Via Romana 53
Santa Margherita (GE) 16038, Italy
tel: (0185) 283431 / 287923 or (0330) 486432
7 rooms with private bathrooms
Lire 90,000 double B&B
  75,000 per person half board
Breakfast and dinner served
Open March-October
Some English spoken
Region: Liguria

As more travelers realize just how short the distances are between destinations of interest throughout Italy, the number of requests for weekly house rentals has increased considerably. Instead of changing B&B's every two days within a region, visitors have easy access to many places from one base that they can call "home." One such ideal base is La Sovana bordering Tuscany and Umbria and equidistant to Florence, Chianti, Siena, Cortona, Perugia, Assisi, plus many other smaller hilltowns. Two stone farmhouses were recently restored to provide 10 different apartment situations for 2-7 persons. Tastefully decorated with local antique beds and armoires, matching floral bedspreads and curtains, they include a fully-equipped kitchenette in travertine and eating area. The dining room in the main house, whose enormous arched window takes in the view of the vast open landscape, is where guests can dine upon request. The cordial Olivi family from Perugia is present on weekends and throughout the summer. Otherwise guests are left in the capable hands of the caretakers. Potted flowers are plentiful around the farmhouse and poolside, where on Saturday nights a welcome barbecue is organized. Tennis courts are also available. *Directions:* Just 2 km from the Chiusi exit, A1 autostrada. La Sovana is just before Sarteano on the right..

LA SOVANA
Hosts: Giuseppe Olivi family
Localita: Sovana
Sarteano (SI) 53047, Italy
tel: (0578) 274086; fax: (075) 600197
10 apartments
Lire 550,000-1,2000,000 weekly
Dinner served upon request
Open Easter-November
Very little English spoken
Region: Tuscany

Saturnia's thermal waters have been gushing from an underground volcano for over 2,000 years, yet only recently have it and the enchanting *maremma* area surrounding it become internationally famous. In response to growing demand, new accommodations have sprung up, including the charming Villa Clodia, once home to nobility, now run by former restaurateur Giancarlo Ghezzi. The villa is a curiosity, seemingly built out of the limestone rock, one side overlooking the street and the other on an expansive valley of grapevines and olive trees. Because of its unusual proportions, each room is unique in size and decor. A small winding stairway takes guests up or down to rooms, some of which have been literally carved out of the rock. All bedrooms feature scattered antiques, new bathrooms and valley views, and a fortunate few boast a terrace. Breakfast is offered in a sweet, luminous room next to the sitting room. A lush rose garden and fruit orchard surround the inviting star-shaped pool. Lots of regular guests makes advance reservations a must and weekly stays are preferred. *Directions:* From Rome take the Aurelia highway north, turning off to the right at Vulci where you follow signs for Manciano, Montemerano and Saturnia. Villa Clodia is in the middle of town.

VILLA CLODIA
Host: Giancarlo Ghezzi
Via Italia 43
Saturnia (GR) 58050, Italy
tel & fax: (0564) 601212
10 rooms with private bathrooms
Lire 110,000 double B&B
3-day minimum stay
Breakfast only
Credit cards: VS
Closed February
English spoken well
Region: Tuscany

At just 20 km from Siena, at the foot of Chianti is the Godiolo stone farmhouse with its double loggia and cupola dating back to 1350. Red geraniums cascade from every one of the balconies and terra-cotta urns. While Signor Giuliano tends to the vineyards and wine-production, Signora Bianca dedicates her time to making their guests feel very much at home. What used to be the children's rooms are now four charming guestrooms with nice touches—embroidered linen sheets and dried flower arrangements. Breakfast in the typical tiled kitchen consists of homemade baked goods which guests help themselves to. Signora, with her Roman-Tuscan origins is an excellent cook and guests can treat themselves to a delightful dinner together with the family. Their son, Stefano, when not studying, is often around to assist and is eager to practice his English. Nearby are the thermal baths of Rapolano where massages, mud baths and other spa services are available—true relaxation. *Directions:* Exit from A1 autostrada at Val di Chiana and head towards Siena on rte. 326 to Serre di Rapolano, but turn right, up to Godiolo rather than left into town.

GODIOLO
Hosts: Giuliano & Bianca Perinelli
Localita: Modanella
Serre di Rapolano, (SI) 53040, Italy
tel: (0577) 704304
4 rooms with private bathrooms
Lire 200,000 double B&B
Dinner served upon request
Open all year
Some English spoken
Region: Tuscany

On the same road as the Godiolo B&B, a more independent type of accommodation is offered at the Castello di Modanella dating back to the 13th Century. It is a sprawling stone complex complete with towers and turrets, several separate houses where the farmers of the vast wine estate once lived, a church and even a school. The castle is in a constant state of restoration and along the way thirteen apartments for rental have been incorporated in various sections. Some apartments can be found in the old schoolhouse on two floors with one, two or three bedrooms, bathrooms, kitchen, and living room. They maintain their true rustic flavor with original beams, mansard ceilings, worn brick floors, stone walls and a mix of old and new wood furniture. All have lovely views over the countryside. Five other comfortable apartments are located down the road within a separate house where the swimming pool and tennis courts are. Although currently there are no accommodations actually in the castle, it is worth a visit—complete with arched entrance, iron gates, stone courtyard and clock tower. The estate is under the direction of Gabriella Cerretti who assists guests with their every need. *Directions:* From Siena on rte 326 towards the autostrada, for 30 km, turn left at sign for the Castello, opposite Serre di Rapolano.

CASTELLO DI MODANELLA
Hostess: Gabriella Cerretti
Serre di Rapolano, (SI) 53040, Italy
tel: (0577) 704604; fax: (0577) 704740
13 apartments for 2-9 persons
Lire 150,00-330,000 daily
2-day minimum stay
No meals served
Open all year
Some English spoken
Region: Tuscany

The Podere Novelleto sits on the summit of the residential suburb of Sesto Fiorentino, above the spellbinding city of Florence, known for its concentration of Medici villas. The stone farmhouse is the last residence on the street to maintain a substantial amount of land under cultivation. Twenty-five hectares of olive groves parade down the hill behind the house, and out front, visitors are treated to a fabulous panorama of red-roofed Florence. Meals are served on an open terrace, strategically oriented to capitalize on the unique view which becomes even more magical at night. Here amidst a grape arbor and potted geraniums, guests may enjoy a delightful Florentine meal. Host Arrigo Luppi provides hospitality in a wing attached to the main house, all of which has been dedicated to that purpose. Five bedrooms with private bath are simply decorated with family antiques, although some are too modern in decor. Only eight km north of Florence, this bed and breakfast is an ideal base from which to explore the region. *Directions:* It is very difficult to find Podere Novelleto. Call from Sesto Fiorentino to be accompanied.

PODERE NOVELLETO
Host: Arrigo Luppi
Via Carmignanello 4—Quinto Alto
Sesto Fiorentino (FI) 50019, Italy
tel: (055) 454056
5 rooms with private bathrooms
Lire 100,000 double B&B
  75,000 per person half board
Breakfast and dinner served
Credit cards: VS
Open all year
Some English spoken
Region: Tuscany

There is a beautiful piece of coastline on the Adriatic Sea just south of Ancona, which differs dramatically from the more flat and uninteresting shoreline to the north and south, where modern hotels and condos proliferate. The quaint stone village of Sirolo sits high above the water on a mountainside looking down to the beaches of the Riviera Conero. Delightful seafood restaurants dot the shore, where you might enjoy a plate of pasta with fresh clams while watching the tide come in. Isabella and Giorgio Fabiani decided several years ago to open a B&B in 14th-century Sirolo, and offer four guest rooms above their small restaurant with its outdoor tables. The bedrooms are simply furnished in old-fashioned style, and most have sea views. The young couple is full of ideas to improve the premises, but being a historical building (legend has it that St. Francis stayed overnight here), even simple renovations are often restricted. No extra bathrooms are allowed—not even the faded green shutters adorning the windows can be touched. Nonetheless, the place exudes a basic charm. Meals are created in true Marchigiano style; natives of the Marches are known for their skill in the preparation of seafood dishes (*brodetto*). *Directions:* The Rocco is located in the town of Sirolo, after Portonovo.

LOCANDA ROCCO
Hostess: Isabella Fabiani
Via Torrione 1
Sirolo (AN) 60020, Italy
tel: (071) 9330558 / 7823256
5 rooms sharing 2 bathrooms
Lire 72,000 double B&B
* 80,000 per person half board*
All meals served
Credit cards: VS, AX, DC
Open April-October
Some English spoken
Region: Marches

The stone tower of Bagnara, dating back nearly a thousand years is situated in the Upper Tiber Valley just 20 km north of Perugia, and not far from the major cultural centers of Umbria, Assisi, Gubbio and Citta del Castello. The independent tower is part of the vast tobacco farm of the Tremi family who reside in a luxurious villa just down the hill. Three fully equipped apartment-suites accommodating two to six people have been fashioned within the tower (available for weekly rental only). The quarters come complete with kitchenette and are nicely furnished in a refined country style with antiques, painted wrought-iron beds, and matching floral curtains and bedspreads. Original architectural features such as beamed ceilings, terra-cotta floors and arched stone doorways, lend authentic medieval ambiance to a stay here. And given the sweeping views it commands over the valley, it's easy to understand why this spot was chosen for a watchtower. The backdrop consists of wooded hills dotted with grazing livestock and distant farmhouses. An excellent and unusual base for thorough exploration of the natural and man-made wonders of this rich region. *Directions:* From Perugia, exit at Ponte Pattoli from highway 45. Follow signs for Umbertide, turning left at the second road, not right for Solfagnano. The Tremi villa is the first on the left.

LA TORRE DI BAGNARA
Hosts: Tremi family
Solfagnano (PG) 06080, Italy
tel: (075) 604136
3 apartments
Lire 700,000-1,300,000 weekly
No meals served
Open March-October
English spoken well
Region: Umbria

The town of Spoleto has gained international fame over the past 20 years thanks to the *Due Mondi* festival in July. It is a series of cultural events including ballet, theater, opera and concerts with renowned artists that lasts an entire month and attracts a worldwide audience. Accommodations are reserved from one year to the next. For the rest of the year, however, Spoleto holds its own along with nearby Assisi, Spello, Todi and Perugia, as an enchanting medieval stone town, rich in historical past. The Vaita de Domo serves as an excellent base from which to explore in-depth the entire region of Umbria. Paolo Tamburi, from Rome, bought and restored the 17th-century palazzo, situated within the old walls of the town, five years ago and created eight spacious apartments for weekly stays. The apartments vary in size and layout, accommodating from 2-7 persons. All take in views over the tiled rooftops and contain 1-3 bedrooms, fully-equipped kitchen, living area and 1 or 2 bathrooms. The largest, number 4, is spread out on three levels. Beds, tables, and armoires were made by a local carpenter and are awaiting decorative touches. For the present, rooms are very comfortable, including all amenities, but rather "unfinished" looking. This should be resolved soon with the arrival of matching bedspreads and curtains and original paintings. Cordial hostess, Daniela, of Spoleto, is on hand to assist guests, including furnishing breakfast supplies upon request. *Directions:* From autostrada A1, exit at Orte and follow rte. 418 to Spoleto. Best to call from town for directions.

RESIDENZA VAITA DE DOMO
Hostess: Daniela Tulli
Via Vaita de Domo 5
Spoleto (PG) 06049, Italy
tel: (06) 44243882; fax: (06) 8557753
8 apartments
Lire 900,000-1,600,000 weekly
No meals served
Open all year
Some English spoken
Region: Umbria

Halfway between Florence and Siena in the heart of the Chianti region is the Sovigliano farm, recently restored by a handsome couple from Verona, Claudio Bicego and his wife, who delight in welcoming international visitors into their warm home. Guests have an independent entrance to the five bedrooms (only two with private bath), each very much in keeping with the pure simplicity of this typical farmhouse. Exposed-beam ceilings and terra-cotta floors, antique beds and armoires and bucolic views make time stand still here. There is also a two-bedroom apartment within the house, decorated in similar style, with kitchen and dining area. The upstairs living room, sparsely furnished with the family's elegant antiques, kitchen with country fireplace and surrounding garden are for everyone's use. Signor Claudio is actively involved in the production of top Tuscan wines in conjunction with several other wine estates, and also coordinates with other area residents to organize lessons in language, history and culinary arts with local professors. *Directions:* From Siena, exit the superstrada at Poggibonsi; from Florence at Tavarnelle. Follow signs for Tavarnelle and, go through town towards Barberino, turning off at sign for Sovigliano.

PODERE SOVIGLIANO
Hosts: Bicego family
Via Magliano 9
Tavarnelle Val di Pesa (FI) 50028, Italy
tel & fax: (055) 8076217
5 rooms, 2 with private bathrooms
1 apartment
Lire 110,000 double B&B
 80,000 per person half board
2-day minimum stay
Dinner upon request
Open all year
English spoken well
Region: Tuscany

Another one of Italy's best-kept secrets is the *Cinque Terre* coastline of southern Liguria bordering Tuscany. The area is gaining increasing attention, and rightfully so as it is beautiful and quite unique. Its five quaint stone villages hugging the hillside sweeping down to the sea, until recently, were accessible only by boat of by foot and are a delight to explore. Just south of the area right on the *Poet's Gulf* is the adorable seaside town of Tellaro, where visitors make a point of stopping to have a memorable meal at the Miranda restaurant. Husband and wife team, Giovanna and Angelo have their own inimitable and ever-varying style of cooking based on fresh seafood which is present in the inexhaustible series of antipasti plates. They certainly deserve every bit of the praise that comes their way. Meals are served either out on the screened-in porch with its green and white awnings, or in one of the three peach-colored dining rooms, simply and pleasantly appointed with scattered antiques. In the same vein are the seven guestrooms which Aunt Miranda used to rent out and are now another part of the Cabani's responsibilities. A perfect base from which to enjoy this lesser-known area. *Directions:* Exit from A12 autostrada at Sarzana, following signs for Lerici on rte 331. Tellaro is 4.5 km down the coast and the Miranda is on the main road before town.

LOCANDA MIRANDA
Hosts: Angelo & Giovanna Cabani
Via Fiascherino 92
Tellaro (SP) 19030, Italy
tel: (0187) 968130 / 964012; fax:(0187) 964032
7 rooms with private bathrooms
Lire 140,000 double B&B
3-day minimum stay
All meals served
Credit cards: all major except AX
Open: March-January
English spoken well
Region: Liguria

You would never happen upon the Residenza San Andrea al Farinaio because it is located so far off the beaten path that you must write or call ahead for detailed instructions if you ever hope to find it. Once you have settled in, however, the location is quite convenient as a home base for exploring both Tuscany and Umbria. And for those looking for well-priced accommodation without sacrificing comfort, this bed and breakfast might be the perfect selection. The oldest part of the inn dates back to the 13th Century when it was home to the priests tending a church which stood across the road. The present owner, Patrizia Nappi, is a warm and gracious hostess, speaks excellent English and has lovingly transformed the old stone house into a cozy inn, combining modern pictures, furniture and knickknacks with lovely antiques. Of the five bedrooms, three have private baths. A personal favorite is the large guest room at the top of the stairs. The most wonderful area in the house is the dining room with its massive darkened-wood beams, large open fireplace, beautiful antique trestle table, colorful plates adorning the walls and lots of copper pots and pans. If you make arrangements in advance, you can dine here with other guests, sharing a simple, superb meal family-style at the long, handsome candlelit table in front of a crackling fire. *Directions:* Head southeast from Cortona to Terontola (approximately 10 km) and follow for Stadio, continue until you see sign on right for S. Andrea.

RESIDENZA SAN ANDREA AL FARINAIO
Hostess: Patrizia Nappi
San Andrea al Farinaio, 118
Terontola di Cortona, (AR) 52040, Italy
tel: (0575) 677736
4 rooms with private bathrooms
Lire 200,000 double B&B
Breakfast and dinner served
Open all year
Fluent English spoken
Region: Tuscany

Practically 70 percent of the families residing in the Alto Adige mountain region offer B&B accommodations so, unless it's Christmas or August, a bed is not hard to come by. This is a region with a distinct Austrian flavor where more German than Italian is spoken, and where more *wurstel* than pasta is likely to be served at the table. The warm Trompedeller family heartily welcome international travelers to their typical Tyrolian-style home. The six guestrooms each have a private bath, and are modestly decorated with basic light-wood furniture and accented with orange and brown curtains and bedspreads—a decor common to the B&B in this region. The cozy wood-paneled dining room boasts a splendid panoramic view over the mountain cliffs and green foothills. The house is located several miles outside the quaint town of Tiers on a road which comes to an end at a babbling brook surrounded by hushed woods with hiking trails. Depending on the season, guests can take advantage of the Val Gardena ski slopes or summer mountain climbing. *Directions:* From the Verona-Brennero autostrada, exit at Bolzano Nord and follow signs for Tiers. Go through the town and make a hairpin left turn at the chapel.

VERALTENHOF
Hosts: Josef Trompedeller family
Oberstrasse 61
Tiers (BZ) 39050, Italy
tel: (0471) 642102
6 rooms with private bathrooms
Lire 40,000 per person half board
Breakfast and dinner served
Open all year
No English spoken
Region: Alto Adige

Since 1830, the 12th-century castle and 4,000-acre farm of Titignano have been among the many properties of the noble Corsini family. Eight years ago the family decided to participate in the increasingly popular agriturismo trade by offering six guestrooms in the main house, and just recently added a swimming pool and 3 new apartments in the what was originally the farmer's quarters. They are pleasantly decorated with scattered country antiques. The undertaking is primarily the responsibility of the Fontanis, a delightful young couple who take care of everything from looking after guests and the farm to cooking and serving. Meals are shared at a long table in one of the castle's graciously neglected rooms with an enormous gray stone fireplace sporting the family coat of arms, and lofty ceilings made of the stamped terra-cotta blocks typical of Umbria. Off the dining hall are the spacious bedrooms, each with modernized pink travertine bathrooms and decorated eclectically with unrefined antiques and wrought-iron beds. They have a worn charm about them. Common areas include a living room with bright floral sofas around a fireplace, a game and TV room for children, and a large terrace with a sweeping view covering three regions that will take your breath away. *Directions:* From the Roma-Firenze A1 autostrada, exit at Orvieto. Follow signs for Arezzo, turning on route 79 for Prodo. Follow long winding road for 35 km past Prodo to Titignano.

FATTORIA TITIGNANO
Hosts: Monica & Giulio Fontani
Localita: Titignano
Orvieto (TR) 05010, Italy
tel & fax: (0763) 308322
6 rooms with private bathrooms, 3 apartments
Lire 100,000 double B&B
* 70,000 per person half board*
Breakfast and dinner served
Open all year
Some English spoken
Region: Umbria

The vast Palazzetta farm, up in the hills outside the picturesque Medieval/Renaissance town of Todi, offers a nice combination of comfortable accommodations along with excellent local fare. The Caracciolo family reside in one of the many farmhouses comprising a complex of 17th-century stone buildings, while guests are accommodated in the converted farmers' quarters, or in the main villa where the most lovely rooms are situated. These rooms have specially selected antiques, stenciled drawings and generous views over the rolling countryside. The original architectural features of the buildings naturally enhance the remaining guestrooms—the stone interior walls, high-beamed ceilings and terra-cotta floors appropriately complementing the simple country antiques. A cozy living room separating the rooms with an enormous fireplace and soft floral sofas invites guests to curl up with a good book. Yet other rooms are divided between the one-story barn and house behind the restaurant (although they are rather small). The former cattle barn is now a delightful restaurant, totally frescoed on one wall by a well-known set designer. One can also dine on the veranda overlooking green hills and distant swimming pool. Here guests are treated to a superb meal prepared by a chef formerly from a famous local restaurant. *Directions:* From Todi follow signs for Orvieto, turning left at the sign for Palazzetta and proceeding for 7 km. From Orvieto, take rte. 448 toward Todi, watching for Palazzetta signs after the lake ends.

LA PALAZZETTA
Hosts: Ennio Caracciolo family
Localita: Asproli
Todi (PG) 06059, Italy
tel: (075) 8853219; fax: (075) 8853358
19 rooms with private bathrooms
Lire 120,000-150,000 double B&B
 (prices seasonal), 3-day minimum stay
All meals served
Open all year
Some English spoken
Region: Umbria

La Dogana means customs house in Italian, and the fascinating history of this 16th-century building—which until 1870 served as the Papal customs house for travelers through the Grand Duchy of Tuscany—boasts visits from luminary artists as Michelangelo, Goethe, Byron and Stendhal. The 100-acre property belongs to young hosts Emanuele and Paola and aside from the main villa, includes a stone farmhouse and a building near the stables across the street. In these two "extra" buildings 25 apartment-suites have been created. The guest quarters vary widely in condition, but all feature a living area, kitchen, bathroom and sleeping accommodations for two to six people. Each apartment is unique in decor, containing mixed antiques, prints, old sofas and wrought-iron beds. Up on a hillside, guests have a lovely view over Lake Trasimeno whose encircling highway is audible even from here. Although no meals are served, the Dogana is conveniently situated near Perugia, Cortona and Montepulciano, where an excellent meal is a cinch to find. *Directions:* From Perugia, take N75 toward Firenze, exiting at Tuoro. Turn left at first intersection, continuing 5 km to La Dogana on the right side of the road.

LA DOGANA
Host: Marchese Emanuele de Ferrari
Via Dogana 4
Tuoro sul Trasimeno, (PG) 06069, Italy
tel: (075) 8230158; fax: (075) 8230252
25 apartments
Lire 350,000-850,000
   weekly (July & August)
No meals served
Open all year
English spoken very well
Region: Umbria

Those who have fallen in love with the enchanting countryside of Tuscany, but found its roads too well-traveled, should investigate the northern part of the Marches surrounding Urbino. The scenery is magnificent, the ancient towns perfectly preserved and the ambiance authentic. The Blasi families, hard-working farmers, have dedicated themselves to balancing a productive farm with a bed and breakfast. The brother's side of the family tends to the fields, while Amadeo, his wife Maria and their two sons see to the guests. Three simple terra-cotta roofed houses make up the farm, and horses, cows, sheep and even peacocks roam the grounds. The eight guestrooms, each with private bath, are spartan, and the decor uninspired, but the familial warmth of the hospitality, the excellent home cooking and the value compensate. In the rustic dining room with red-checked tablecloths or on the windowed veranda overlooking the gently rolling, wooded countryside, guests indulge in Maria's spinach ravioli or hand-cut tagliatelle, fresh-baked bread and local wine. *Directions:* From Urbino take the road to Urbania. Pass through town and follow signs for Acqualagna. After 9 km turn right where indicated and follow signs up to L'Orsaiola.

L'ORSAIOLA
Hosts: Blasi families
Localita: Orsaiola
Urbania 61049 (PS) 61049, Italy
tel: (0722) 318988
5 rooms, 2 with private bathrooms
2 apartments
Lire 50,000 double B&B
* 50,000 per person half board*
All meals served
Open March to Christmas
Very little English spoken
Region: Marches

Isabella and her husband came down from the Dolomite mountains to the enchanting area surrounding the town of Urbino 20 years ago and have resided there ever since. Their stone farmhouse is situated on the summit of one of the rolling green hills that characterize this bucolic countryside here. Before starting the B&B, Isabella had her own esthetician business and continues to practice that trade by offering her guests facials and massages with her own natural herbal creams; hence the name *Beauty Farm*. Guests are made to feel right at home at the Giuriatti's, sharing the spacious living room, well-furnished with family antiques, and dining room where meals are enjoyed all together at a big table. As the cook is from Sardinia, specialties served are not specific to the Marches. However, one regional delicacy often figures in the dishes, since part of the farm is a white-truffle reserve. Upstairs are found the five guestrooms, each with bath, casually and individually arranged using a mix of old and new furniture and personal family items. Besides the beautiful university town of Urbino, there are other interesting side trips to nearby San Leo and the Republic of San Marino. *Directions:* From Urbino (10 km) take route 73 toward Arezzo. After Montesoffio turn right at Pozzuolo.

THE BEAUTY FARM
Hostess: Isabella Giuriati
Localita: Pozzuolo 60-Montesoffio
Urbino, (PS) 61029, Italy
tel: (0722) 57183
5 rooms with private bathrooms
Lire 100,000 double B&B
*   70,000 per person half board*
Breakfast and dinner served
Open all year
Some English spoken
Region: Marches

The recently opened Brombolona Inn was discovered by chance in the back hills of Urbino. Benny and his wife Lucia, natives of the area and long-time owners of the renowned *Nuovo Coppiere* restaurant in town, knew what they were doing when they purchased and painstakingly restored this 15th-century stone "castle." Perched atop a small mountain, surrounded by national park, it offers 360-degree panoramas from virtually every window. Gregarious Benny's dream has been realized with the completion of the inn: a home in an idyllic setting where friends old and new can visit and be assured of absolute repose. The eighteen comfortable rooms with bath are furnished in a modern and functional fashion lacking obvious charm. The views and Lucia's superb fresh cuisine compensate. Truffles are the local specialty. Benny's enthusiasm for the area is contagious and he soon has guests on outings to his favorite spots (the old mill, bell tower, abandoned convent), enhancing them with his substantial historical knowledge. When asked how many "stars" his inn has, his answer is that the only stars he knows of blanket the black sky over his beloved Brombolona. *Directions:* From Urbino (18 km) take road to Fossombrone, turn left at Brombolona sign and follow winding road to the end.

LOCANDA BROMBOLONA
Hosts: Lucia & Benny Nicoli
Localita: Sant' Andrea in Primicilio
Canavaccio di Urbino (PS) 61029, Italy
tel & fax: (0722) 53501
12 rooms with private bathrooms
Lire 96,000 double B&B
All meals served
Credit card: MC
Open all year
Some English spoken
Region: Marches

The Gasthof Obereggen, located in the Ega Valley is very simple, but its location and price are hard to match. The inn is situated on the side of a hill overlooking a gorgeous valley in one of the most beautiful mountain regions of northeastern Italy. The town of Obereggen is a ski resort and the lift is just a few minutes' walk away. From the sun-drenched deck, which extends generously from the hotel, there is an absolutely glorious vista across the meadows to the mountains. Behind the hotel even more majestic peaks rise jaggedly into the sky. Inside there is a cozy dining room. Signor Pichler must be a hunter, for trophies line the walls, and there is a typical tiled stove against one wall to keep the room toasty on a cold day. The inn has twelve basically uninspired bedrooms, with those on the second floor opening out onto balconies with lovely views. The Gasthof's greatest asset is Signora Pichler. She is very special, running her little inn with warmth and gaiety. Signora Pichler speaks no English, but her hospitality overcomes all language barriers, and her abundant and delicious home-style cooking speaks to all who love to eat. *Directions:* Obereggen is almost impossible to find on any map, although the Val d'Ega and the town of Ega (San Floriano on some maps) are usually indicated. Obereggen is three km south of Nova Levante and 25 km southeast of Bolzano.

GASTHOF OBEREGGEN
Hosts: Pichler family
Obereggen (San Floriano)
Val d'Ega (BZ) 39050, Italy
tel: (0471) 615722
12 rooms several with private bathrooms
Lire 60,000 per person half board
All meals served
Closed May-June
No English spoken (German)
Region: Alto Adige

Varenna is a quaint little village sitting halfway up Lake Como's eastern edge. It is situated at the point where the car-ferryboats cross over to the other side of the lake to Menaggio. In the main piazza lakeside is the family-run Olivedo hotel with its pale yellow facade. Time seems to have stood still within its old-fashioned interior. The reception area and side bar are dressed with faded floral wallpaper, scattered antiques and a large grandfather clock chiming the hour. Off to the other side of the reception area is a dining room/restaurant with its simple frescoes, serving all meals. A curved stairway takes guests up to the 19 rooms most with ensuite bathroom and lake views. These are decorated simply with grandmother's furniture and old prints. There is no need to worry about noise since traffic is not allowed in the piazza. *Directions:* From Como branch of lake, head north on either side of lake and take the ferry over from either Bellagio or Menaggio.

OLIVEDO
Hosts: Colombo family
Varenna (CO) 22050, Italy
tel: (0341) 830115
19 rooms, 10 with private bathrooms
Lire 85,000 double B&B
All meals served
Open all year
Very little English spoken
Region: Lombard

At first glance the exterior of the Pensione Seguso appears quite bland: a rather boxy affair with few of the elaborate architectural enhancements so frequently evident in Venice. Inside, however, the *pensione* radiates warmth and charm, with oriental rugs setting off antique furniture and an heirloom silver service. The hotel is located on the "left bank" of Venice: across the Grand Canal from the heart of the tourist area, about a 15-minute walk to St Mark's Square (or only a few minutes by ferry from the Accademia boat stop). For several generations the hotel has been in the Seguso family, which provides a homey ambiance for guests who do not demand luxury. In front there is a miniature terrace harboring a few umbrella-shaded tables. Several of the bedrooms have views of the canal (although these are the noisiest due to canal traffic). Being a simple *pensione*, most of the rooms share a bathroom, so if you are looking for hotel amenities, Seguso may not be your "cup of tea." The pleasant surprise is that the value-conscious tourist can stay here with breakfast and dinner included for the price of a room alone at most Venice hotels. *Directions:* The Seguso is a 10-minute walk from the Accademia boat stop.

PENSIONE SEGUSO
Hosts: Lorenzo Seguso family
Grand Canal Zattere 779
Venice 30123, Italy
tel: (041) 5286858; fax: (041) 5222340
36 rooms, 19 with private bathrooms
Lire 120,000 per person half board
Breakfast and dinner served
Credit cards: all major
Open March-November
English spoken well
Region: Veneto

An outstanding alternative to the city hotels of Venice is the perfectly charming Gargan B&B situated in the countryside just 40km from Venice. The Calzavara family from the lovely city of Treviso renovated the family's expansive 17th-century country house and opened the B&B with restaurant just three years ago. Guests are offered four sweetly decorated bedrooms each with their own bathroom on the top floor. Signora Calzavara enjoys making her guests feel as "at home" as possible by having fresh flowers in the already cozy, antique-filled bedrooms. The downstairs sitting and dining rooms display the family's country antiques as well as a large fireplace and nice touches such as lace curtains and paintings. Guests are treated to a full breakfast of homebaked cakes and exceptional 5-course dinners prepared by daughter-in-law Anna who insists on using all ingredients from their farm. Guests will be fascinated watching her prepare her own pastas and breads in the family kitchen. Meanwhile, son, Alessandro oversees the farm activity and horses. The Gargan is an ideal choice in the Veneto region because it is a short drive from such marvels as Padova, Venice, Treviso, Vicenza and Verona. *Directions:* From Venice take the Rte 245 to Scorze then follow signposts to Levada (outside the town of Piombino Dese). A local train is available from Padova.

GARGAN
Hosts: Calzavara Family
Via Marco Polo 2
Levada di Piombino Dese (PD) 35017, Italy
tel: (049) 9350308
4 rooms with private bathrooms
Lire 77,000 double B&B
* 85,000 per person half board*
All meals served
Open all year
Some English spoken
Region: Veneto

Halfway along the shore of Lake Maggiore, at the point where the road curves back down to Verbania, is a farmhouse ideally situated 700 meters above the lake. It commands a 360-degree view which includes the Alps and Lakes Mergozzo, Monate, Varese and Maggiore with its miniature Borromeo islands (accessible by ferryboat). Just 20 km from the Swiss border, it makes a convenient and picturesque stopover on your way into or out of Italy. A 5 km road winds up to the turn-of-the-century house with a tower. Energetic and friendly hostess, Iside Minotti, and her family run the inn and rustic restaurant, which is busy spot in the summer when locals come up to dine and take advantage of the cooler air and the spectacular view. Menu ingredients come directly from the vegetable garden and orchards to the kitchen, where sumptuous local specialties are prepared. Even Papa Minotti gets involved and can be heard singing folk songs in front of the open grill. The 25-acre farm includes riding stables where guests can borrow a horse for a ride through the woods, or the hotel can arrange for a helicopter from Fondotoce, for a breathtakingly scenic ride over the lake. Six basic and modern, though comfortable, double rooms with bath are available for overnight guests. *Directions:* Before Verbania, at Pallanza, take Via Azari to Monterosso (left turnoff) up winding road.

IL MONTEROSSO
Hostess: Iside Minotti
Cima Monterosso-C.P. 13
Verbania (NO) 28050, Italy
tel: (0323) 556510
4 rooms with private bathrooms
Lire 65,000 double B&B
 60,000 per person half board
All meals served
Open all year
Some English spoken
Region: Piedmont

With great finesse, determined partners Paolo and Andrea, an editor and a renowned chef, respectively, managed to purchase this magnificent Renaissance villa—no easy feat, considering the property had been in one family for 700 years. The pale-yellow villa with handsome lawns and surrounding cypress woods commands a spectacular view over the immense valley and Mugello mountain range. This is the area north of Florence known for its concentration of Medici villas. The 8 guestrooms have been restored to their original splendor, with high Florentine woodworked ceilings, carefully selected antiques and delightful blue-and-white-tiled bathrooms. The honeymoon suite features a grand gold-crowned red canopy bed. The entry leads directly to the frescoed dining rooms where Andrea performs his culinary magic. Original combinations of fresh local produce are served with great attention to detail, accompanied by an excellent selection of wines. Recent additions include five new rooms next door to the villa in a separate farmhouse, a lovely swimming pool, and horse stables. Villa Campestri offers refined and romantic accommodations at an exceptional rate. *Directions:* Exit at Barberino di Mugello from A1 autostrada and follow signs for S. Pietro Asieve, then Cardetole, then Sagginale, and finally up the road on the right to Vicchio—35 km from Florence.

VILLA CAMPESTRI
Host: Paolo Pasquali
Localita: Campestri 19/22
Vicchio di Mugello (FI) 50039, Italy
tel: (055) 8490107; fax: (055) 8490108
13 rooms with private bathrooms
Lire 152,000 double B&B
* 110,000 per person half board*
Breakfast & dinner served
Credit cards: VS, MC
Open April-December
English spoken well
Region: Tuscany

Once you have visited La Volpaia you will understand why a young American writer who came as a guest, transferred herself, and remained for three years. This is indeed a special place, thanks to hosts: Silvia, who shares responsibility for running the place with sculptor Andrea Taliaco, a native Roman who bought and restored the 16th-century villa and farm eight years ago. Guests are made to feel welcome from the moment they arrive. Ten tastefully decorated rooms, all with bath, are divided between the main house and a farmhouse down the hill at poolside, and each offers splendid views of the lush Chianti hills. The rooms are furnished with pretty country antiques and floral bedspreads and curtains. Nine groomed horses are available for excursions into the surrounding Tuscan countryside. When international guests sit down together for one of the exquisite meals, accompanied by the Volpaia's own Chianti, conversation is never lacking. It is no wonder that guests return again and again to this idyllic spot. *Directions:* Take the superstrada north from Siena and exit at Poggibonsi, following signs for Barberino. Pass through Vico d'Elsa and turn left onto driveway indicating Volpaia.

LA VOLPAIA
Host: Andrea Taliaco
Strada di Pastine
Vico d'Elsa (FI) 50050, Italy
tel: (055) 8073063; fax: (055) 8073070
10 rooms with private bathrooms
Lire 125,000 per person half board
Breakfast and dinner served
Open all year
English spoken well
Region: Tuscany

On the northern outskirts of the beautiful city of Treviso, which combines a rich historical center with a thriving industrial base (it is home to *Benetton*), is a busy farm which was once a convent. The long building has been made into several residences, one belonging to the two Milani brothers, where a restaurant and six bedrooms have been fashioned for guests. All of the bedrooms have private baths, and their decor is very much in keeping with the simple country style of the farm. Typical Venetian antiques enhance the rooms, which also feature homey touches such as white-lace curtains and soft floral armchairs. Guests can observe the wine production taking place on the farm and are also welcome to take horses out on excursions, or take riding lessons if desired. The restaurant, which is popular with locals as well, prides itself on serving local specialties prepared with the farm's fresh produce and game. The restaurant with its large, open central hearth, is a welcoming gathering spot, decorated with lots of pictures, brass pots, pink tablecloths and fresh flowers. Although the surrounding flat countryside is the not most inspiring, this a great base from which to visit Venice, Padova, Vianza and Verona. *Directions:* From Venice (34 km away), take route N13 through Treviso, and on toward Villorba, turning left at the sign for the Podere. Or exit at Treviso Nord from the A27.

PODERE DEL CONVENTO
Host: Renzo Milani
Via IV Novembre 16
Villorba (TV) 31050, Italy
tel: (0422) 920044 or 920422
6 rooms with private bathrooms
Lire 80,000 double B&B
65,000 per person half board
All meals served
Open all year
Credit cards: AX, VS
No English spoken
Region: Veneto

Ninni Bacchi has done wonders in transforming her family's 300-acre tobacco and grain farm (just 38 km from Orvieto) into a very comfortable bed and breakfast, offering visitors the opportunity to stay in an area that was once the heart of the Etruscan civilization—Tarquinia, Tuscania. Arriving guests are warmly received in the luminous, open living room furnished with antiques surrounding a grand fireplace. Downstairs (where livestock once dwelled) is the large, arcaded restaurant dating back to the 15th Century, where guests can enjoy the fine cuisine of the Lazio region at any meal. Or diners can opt to eat outdoors by the saltwater pool. The five bedrooms off the courtyard in the main house have the most character with architectural features intact, while the remaining 15 suites are lined up in two cottage-like wings, and are more spacious and modern in decor. Ninni has also worked wonders with landscaping, which pleasingly distracts the eye from the rather bland and flat countryside surrounding Viterbo. Unfortunately, the commercial zone of Viterbo is slowly invading the area, so don't be alarmed by the unattractive approach. Tennis, biking and horse back riding, plus the nearby thermal spa are some of the activities offered to guests. Directions: From Rome (120 km away) follow signs for Viterbo. Take Cassia road north of Viterbo 3 km toward Montefiascone, turning right at the Rinaldone sign.

RESIDENCE RINALDONE
Hostess: Ninni Bacchi
Strada Rinaldone, 9-S.S. Cassia km 86
Viterbo 01100, Italy
tel: (0761) 352137; fax: (0761) 353116
5 rooms, 15 suites with private bathrooms
Lire 130,000-150,000 double B&B
Minimum 2-day stay
Credit cards: all major
All meals served
Open April-November
Some English spoken
Region: Lazio

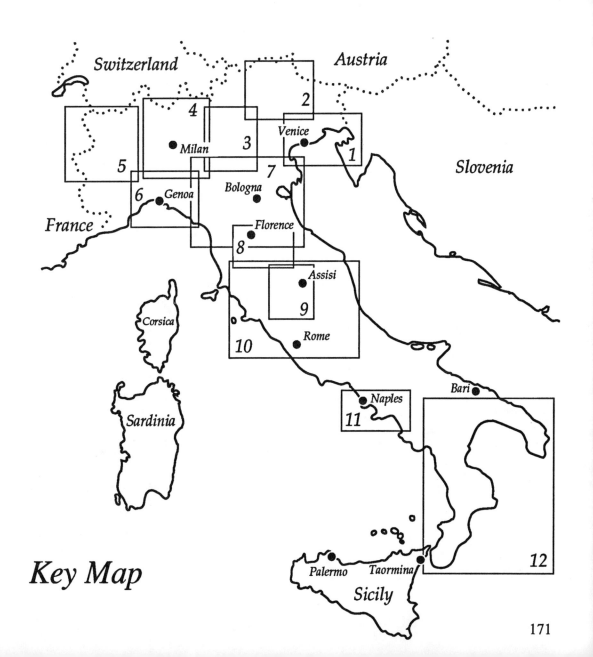

Key Map

171

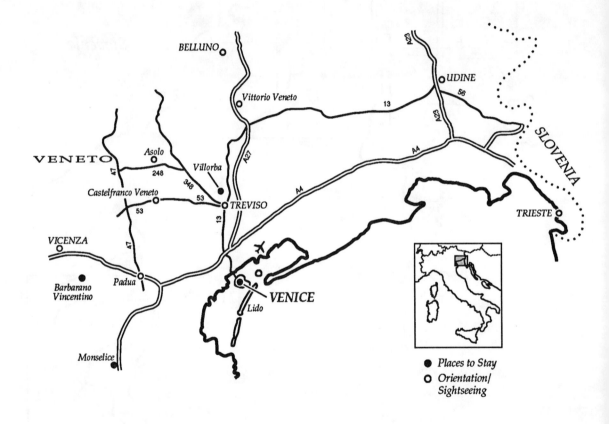

BELLUNO ○

Vittorio Veneto ○

A23

○ UDINE

13

56

A23

SLOVENIA

A27

A4

VENETO

Asolo ○

248

Villorba

348

53

Castelfranco Veneto ○

53

TREVISO ○

13

A4

TRIESTE ○

VICENZA ○

47

Barbarano
Vincentino ●

Padua ○

VENICE

Lido

Monselice ●

● Places to Stay
○ Orientation/
   Sightseeing

Map 1

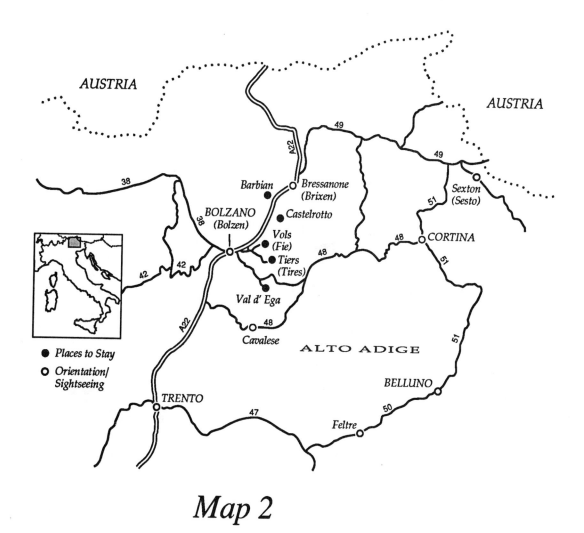

Map 2

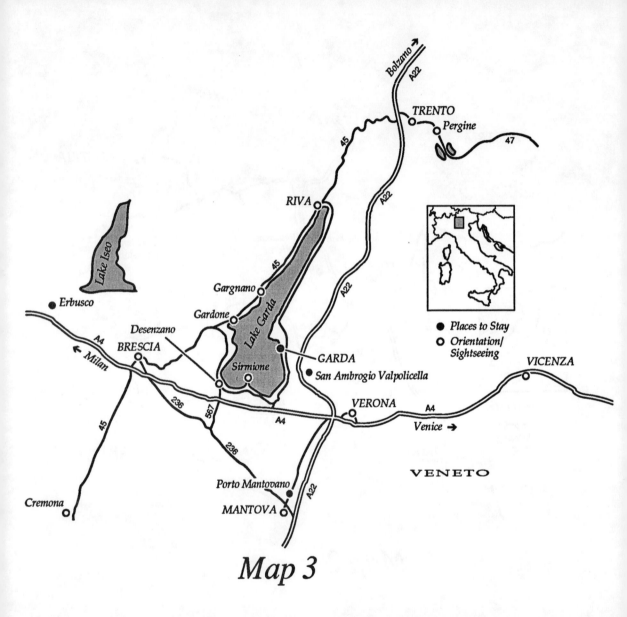

Map 3

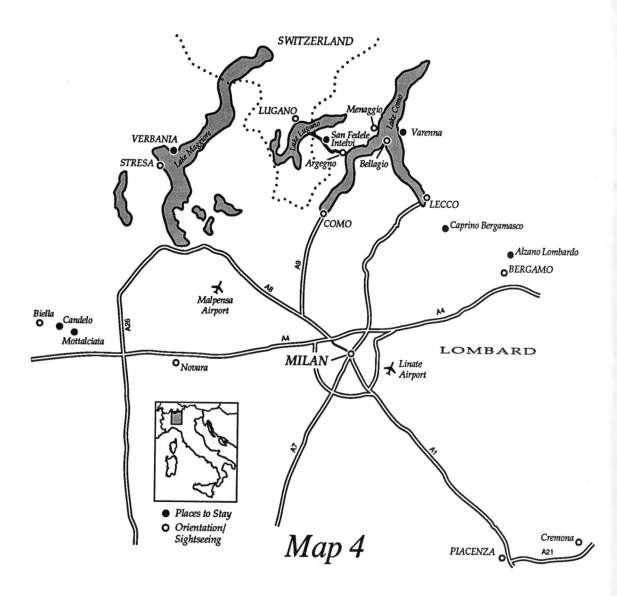

SWITZERLAND

VERBANIA

STRESA

Lake Maggiore

LUGANO

Lake Lugano

Menaggio

Lake Como

San Fedele
Intelvi

Varenna

Argegno

Bellagio

COMO

LECCO

Caprino Bergamasco

A9

Alzano Lombardo

BERGAMO

A8

Malpensa
Airport

A4

Biella

Candelo

Mottalciata

A26

M4

Novara

MILAN

Linate
Airport

LOMBARD

A7

A1

● Places to Stay
○ Orientation/
  Sightseeing

Map 4

PIACENZA

Cremona

A21

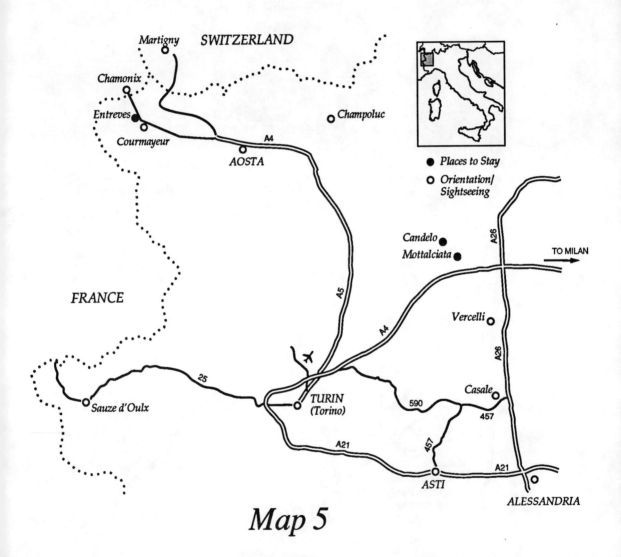

Map 5

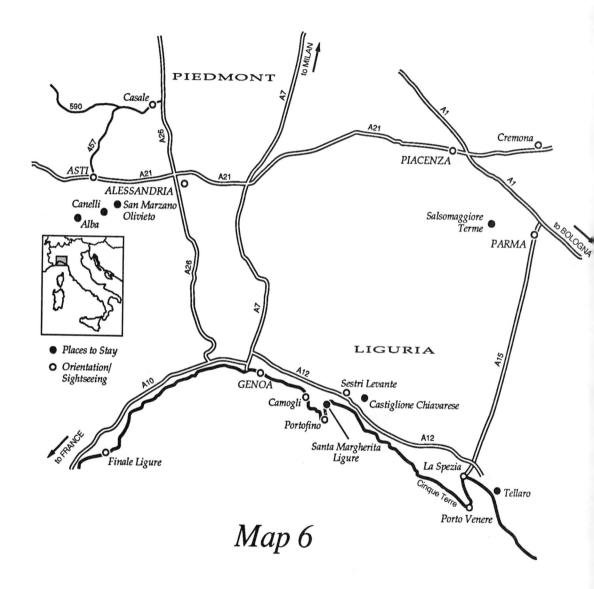

Map 6

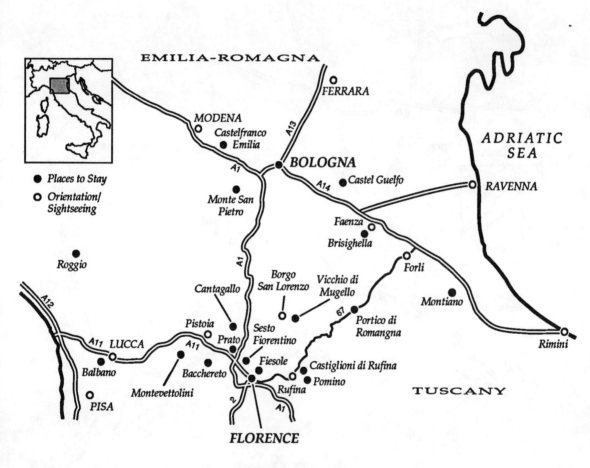

Map 7

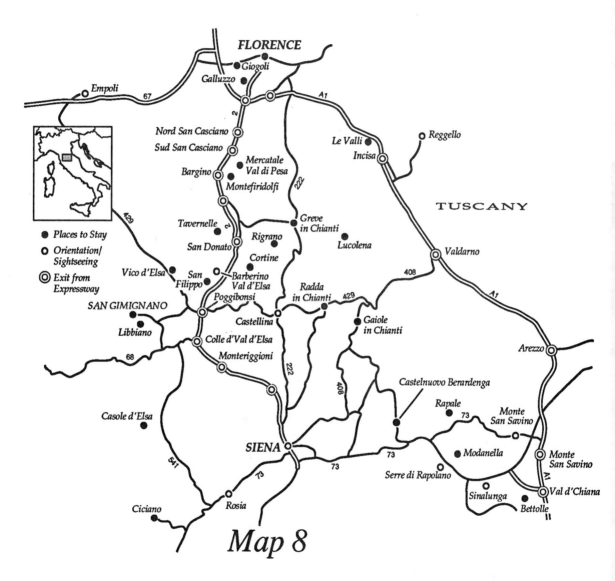

Map 8

Map 9

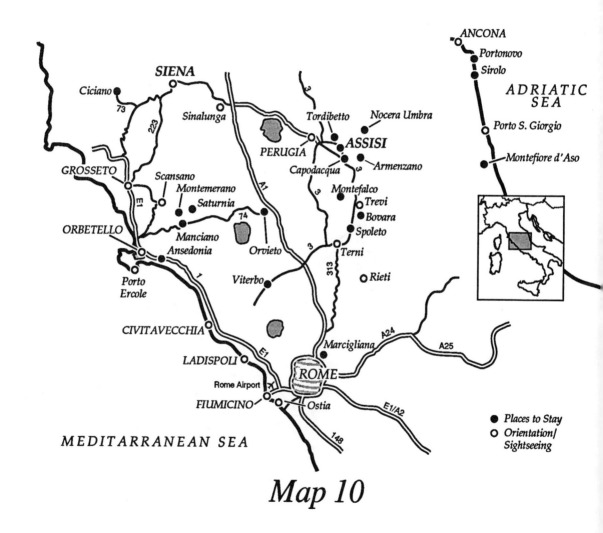

Map 10

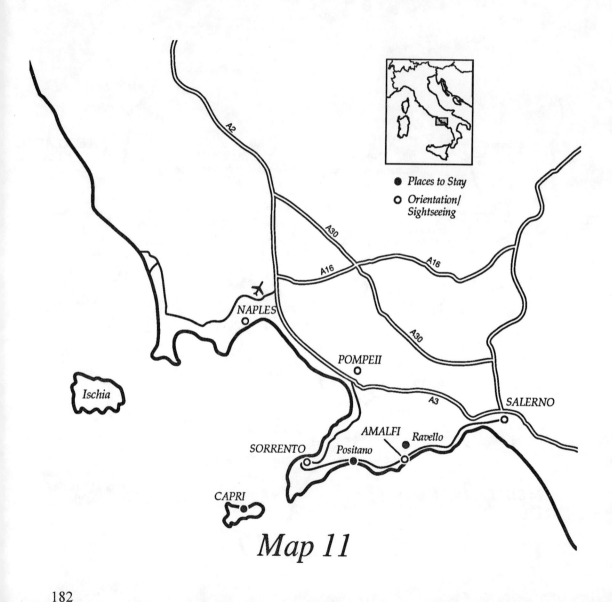

Map 11

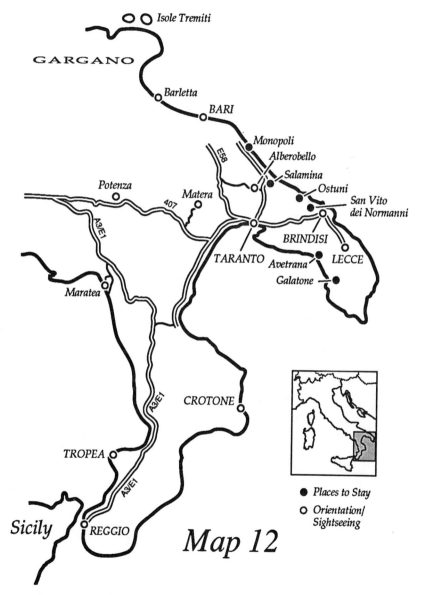

Isole Tremiti

GARGANO

Barletta

BARI

E58

Monopoli

Alberobello

Salamina

Potenza

Matera

Ostuni

407

San Vito
dei Normanni

A3/E1

BRINDISI

TARANTO

Avetrana

LECCE

Maratea

Galatone

A3/E1

CROTONE

A3/E1

TROPEA

Sicily

REGGIO

Map 12

● Places to Stay

○ Orientation/
  Sightseeing

HOTEL RESERVATION REQUEST—LETTER IN ITALIAN

HOTEL NAME & ADDRESS—clearly printed or typed

Vi prego di voler riservare:
I would like to request:

      Numero delle camere con bagno o doccia privata   _____
      Number of rooms with private bath or shower

      Numero delle camere senza bagno o doccia   _____
      Number of rooms without private bath or shower

      Data di arrivo _____ Data di partenza _____
      Date of arrival   *Date of departure*

Vi prego inoltre de fornirmi le seguenti informazioni:
Please let me know as soon as possible the following:

      Potete riservare le camere richieste?   Si / No
      Can you reserve the space requested?   *Yes / No*

      I pasti sono compresi nel prezzo?   Si / No
      Are meals included in your rate?   *Yes / No*

      E necessario un deposito?   Si / No
      Do you need a deposit?   *Yes / No*

      Prezzo giornaliero   _____
      Price per night

      Quanto e necessario come deposito?   _____
      How much deposit do you need?

Ringraziando anticipatamente, porgo distinti saluti,
Thanking you in advance, I send my best regards,

YOUR NAME & ADDRESS—clearly printed or typed

Index

A

B

I

Il Bacchino, 56
Il Castello, 29
Il Covone, 104
Il Monterosso, 166
Il Palazzo, 38
Il Paretaio, 31
Incisa Val d'Arno
    San Niccolo d'Olmeto, 79
Information on Italy, 14
Italia, Casa, 55
Italian Government Travel Offices, 14

K

Krupp, Villa, 43

L

La Casella, 60
La Chiara di Prumiano, 32
La Fenice, 110
La Grange, 57
La Mandria, 39
La Mongolfiera, 58
La Palazzina, 118
La Saracina, 102
La Sosta ai Busini, 54
La Sovana, 144
Language, 5
Le Selve II, 114
Le Silve di Armenzano, 25
Letter in Italian
    Hotel Reservation Request, 185
Levada-Venice
    Gargan, 165

Libbiano, Casolare di, 137
Locanda Borgo Antico, 77
Locanda Brombolona, 161
Locanda Della Rocca, 100
Locanda di Ansedonia, La, 22
Locanda la Bandita, 35
Locanda Laudomia, 91
Locanda Rocco, 149
Locanda Solarola, 47
Locarno, Hotel, 127
Loggia, Fattoria la, 88
Luna e i Falo, La, 40

M

Maiano, Fattoria di, 69
Malvarina, 23
Manciano
    Campigliola Country Club, 80
Mandria, La, 39
Map—Key Map for Hotel Locations, 171
Maps, 10
Maps showing hotel locations, 172, 173, 174, 175, 176, 177, 178, 179, 180, 181, 182, 183
Maria, Villa, 121
Maridiana, La, 95
Marmsolerhof, 51
Masseria Curatori, 82
Masseria lo Prieno, 73
Masseria lo Spagnulo, 99
Masseria Salamina, 59
Meals, 5
Mercatale Val di Pesa
    Salvadonica, 81
Merlhof, 61
Milione, Il, 71

DISCOVERIES FROM OUR READERS

If you have a favorite hideaway that you would be willing to share with other readers, we would love to hear from you. The type of accommodations we feature are those with old-world ambiance, special charm, historical interest, attractive setting, and, above all, warmth of welcome. Please send the following information:

Your name, address, and telephone number.

Name, address, and telephone number of your discovery.

Rate for a double room including tax, service, and breakfast

Brochure or picture (we cannot return material).

Permission to use an edited version of your description.

Would you want your name, city, and state included in the book?

Please send information to:

KAREN BROWN'S GUIDES
Post Office Box 70, San Mateo, CA 94401, USA
Telephone: (415) 342-9117   Fax: (415) 342-9153

Karen Brown's Country Inn Guides

The Most Reliable & Informative Series on Country Inns

Detailed itineraries guide you through the countryside. Every recommendation, from the most deluxe hotel to a simple B&B, is personally inspected, approved and chosen for its romantic ambiance and warmth of welcome. Our charming accommodations reflect every price range, from budget hideaways to the most luxurious palaces.

Order Form for Shipments within the U.S.A.

Please ask in your local bookstore for KAREN BROWN'S GUIDES. If the books you want are unavailable, you may order directly from the publisher.

California Country Inns & Itineraries $14.95

English Country Bed & Breakfasts $13.95

English, Welsh & Scottish Country Hotels & Itineraries $14.95

French Country Bed & Breakfasts $13.95

French Country Inns & Itineraries $14.95

German Country Inns & Itineraries $14.95

Irish Country Inns & Itineraries $14.95

Italian Country Bed & Breakfasts $14.95

Italian Country Inns & Itineraries $14.95

Portuguese Country Inns & Pousadas (1990 edition) $6.00

Spanish Country Inns & Itineraries $14.95

Swiss Country Inns & Itineraries $14.95

Name _____ Street _____

City _____ State ____ Zip _____ Tel: _____

Credit Card (MasterCard or Visa) _____ Exp: _____

Add $3.50 for the first book and .50 cents for each additional book for postage & packing. California residents add 8.25% sales tax. *Order form only for shipments within the U.S.A.*
Indicate number of copies of each title; send form with check or credit card information to:

KAREN BROWN'S GUIDES
Post Office Box 70, San Mateo, California, 94401, U.S.A.
Tel: (415) 342-9117   Fax: (415) 342-9153

HIDDEN TREASURES OF ITALY
Reservation Request Form

Name(s) of traveler(s):_____

Total number in party: _____   Number of children: _____   Ages: _____

Address: _____

_____

Tel: _____

Fax: _____

B&B name and location: _____

Second choice: _____

Type of accommodation: single _____ double _____ triple _____ apt._____

Dates desired: (Arrival) _____   (Departure) _____

Number of nights: _____

Meal plan: B&B _____ half board _____ full board _____ does not apply _____

Special Requests:

HIDDEN TREASURES OF ITALY

Bed & Breakfast Booking Service

You may conveniently reserve any of the B&Bs in this guide through the author Nicole Franchini's booking service. Car rentals and special interest tours (cooking classes, wine tours, or horseback riding excursions) for small groups can also be arranged. Simply copy (as many times as necessary) and fill out the reservation-request form opposite this page and fax or mail it along with a $35 booking fee per B&B (refundable *ONLY* in the case where neither first nor second choices are available) to:

HIDDEN TREASURES OF ITALY
934 Elmwood Avenue
Wilmette, IL 60091
Telephone and Fax: (708) 853-1312

From Europe
Telephone: (Italy) (06) 4424.3882, Fax: (Italy) (06) 855.7753

Upon confirmation of your request(s), exact rates with current exchange rate will be quoted and full prepayment by check or money order will be required within 15 days from the date of notification. After receipt of payment, a written voucher will be issued to you to present to the B&B upon arrival.

CANCELLATION AND CHANGE POLICY

We will do our best to accommodate changes in dates or B&B choice, however this can never be guaranteed. Each additional request will require a supplementary $35 booking fee. Full refund of prepayment (excluding the booking fee) will be given up to 30 days prior to arrival date. No refund will be made within 30 days of your arrival.

Cancellation insurance is strongly recommended

NICOLE FRANCHINI, author of *Italian Country Bed & Breakfasts* was born in Chicago and raised in a bilingual family, her father being Italian. She received a B.A. degree in languages from William Smith College and the Sorbonne, Paris, and has been residing in Italy for the past eight years. Currently living in Rome, she runs her own travel consulting business, Hidden Treasures of Italy, which organizes specialized group and individual itineraries. Nicole also represents several hotels and B&Bs.

ELISABETTA FRANCHINI, the talented artist responsible for the illustrations in *Italian Country Bed & Breakfasts*, lives in her hometown of Chicago where she paints predominantly European landscapes and architectural scenes. This year, on her annual trip abroad, she enjoyed touring Italy with her sister, Nicole Franchini, for their collaborative Bed & Breakfast research for this guide. A Smith College graduate in Art History and French Literature, Elisabetta has exhibited extensively in the Chicago area for the past eight years, and is currently showing her work through a San Francisco gallery.

JANN POLLARD, the artist responsible for the painting on the cover of this guide, has studied art since childhood, and is well-known for her outstanding impressionistic-style water colors which she has exhibited in numerous juried shows, winning many awards. Jann travels frequently to Europe (using Karen Brown's guides) where she loves to paint old world architecture. Jann lives in the San Francisco Bay area with her husband, Gene, and two daughters.

Karen Brown's
Italian Country Inns & Itineraries

The Choice of the Discriminating Traveller to Italy
Featuring the Finest Places to Stay with Charm, and
Detailed Itineraries for Exploring the Countryside

Karen Brown's *Italian Country Inns & Itineraries* is the perfect companion to her *Italian Country Bed & Breakfasts.* Whereas the bed & breakfast guide has "hand-picked" the choice places to stay in private homes, the Italian Country Inns & Itineraries book features accommodations with great charm in small hotels and inns. All the pertinent information is given including: detailed description of accommodation, sketches, price, driving directions, maps, if there is a restaurant, owner's name, telephone and fax number, dates open, etc.

KAREN BROWN'S

ITALIAN

Country Inns & Itineraries

UPDATED AND REVISED • FIFTH EDITION

Italian Country Inns & Itineraries does not replace *Italian Country Bed & Breakfasts*—together they make the perfect pair for the traveler who wants to explore the countryside of Italy. Both feature places to stay with charm, warmth of welcome, and old world ambiance. *Italian Country Bed & Breakfasts* features places to stay in private homes. *Italian Country Inns & Itineraries* features small hotels and inns plus adds five itineraries. Each book has identical detailed maps, making it easy to use both books in combination to select a rich variety of places to spend the night.

SEAL COVE INN—LOCATED IN THE SAN FRANCISCO AREA

Karen Brown Herbert (best known as author of the Karen Brown's Guides) and her husband, Rick, have put seventeen years of experience into reality and opened their own superb hideaway, Seal Cove Inn. Spectacularly set amongst wild flowers and bordered by towering cypress trees, Seal Cove Inn looks out to the ocean over acres of county park: an oasis where you can enjoy secluded beaches, explore tide-pools, watch frolicking seals, and follow the tree-lined path that traces the windswept ocean bluffs. Country antiques, original-watercolors, flower-laden cradles, rich fabrics, and the gentle ticking of grandfather clocks create the perfect ambiance for a foggy day in front of the crackling log fire. Each bedroom is its own haven with a cozy sitting area before a wood-burning fireplace and doors opening onto a private balcony or patio with views to the distant ocean. Moss Beach is a 35-minute drive south of San Francisco, 6 miles north of the picturesque town of Half Moon Bay, and a few minutes from Princeton harbor with its colorful fishing boats and restaurants. Seal Cove Inn makes a perfect base for whale-watching, salmon-fishing excursions, day trips to San Francisco, exploring the coast, or, best of all, just a romantic interlude by the sea, time to relax and be pampered. Karen and Rick look forward to the pleasure of welcoming you to their hide-away by the sea.

Seal Cove Inn, 221 Cypress Avenue, Moss Beach, California, 94038, U.S.A.
telephone: (415) 728-7325   fax: (415) 728-4116